THE
CUBA
PROJECT

THE
CUBA
PROJECT

CASTRO,
KENNEDY,
DIRTY BUSINESS,
DOUBLE DEALING, AND
THE FBI'S TAMALE SQUAD

PETER PAVIA

First published 2006 by
PALGRAVE MACMILLAN™
175 Fifth Avenue, New York, N.Y. 10010 and
Houndmills, Basingstoke, Hampshire, England RG21 6XS.
Companies and representatives throughout the world.

PALGRAVE MACMILLAN IS THE GLOBAL ACADEMIC IMPRINT OF
THE PALGRAVE MACMILLAN division of St. Martin's Press, LLC and
of Palgrave Macmillan Ltd. Macmillan® is a registered trademark in
the United States, United Kingdom and other countries. Palgrave is
a registered trademark in the European Union and other countries.

ISBN 1-4039-6603-6

Library of Congress Cataloging-in-Publication Data

Pavia, Peter, 1959–
    The Cuba project : Castro, Kennedy, and the FBI's Tamale Squad /
Peter Pavia.
        p. cm.
    Includes bibliographical references and index.
    ISBN 1-4039-6603-6 (alk. paper)
        1. United States—Foreign relations—Cuba.   2. Cuba—Foreign
relations—United States.   3. United States—Foreign relations—
1953–1961.   4. United States—Foreign relations—1961–1963.
5. Subversive activities—Cuba—History—20th century.
6. Kennedy, John F. (John Fitzgerald), 1917–1963.   7. Castro, Fidel,
1926–   8. United States. Federal Bureau of Investigation—
History—20th century.   I. Title.

E183.8.C9P375   2006
327.730729109'045—dc22

2005057423

A catalogue record for this book is available from the British Library.

Design by Letra Libre

First edition: March 2006
10 9 8 7 6 5 4 3 2 1
Printed in the United States of America

This Book is For Aunt Fray
Much Love Always

Write down the vision clearly on the tablets,
so that one can read it readily.
For the vision still has its time
presses on to fulfillment,
and will not disappoint;
if it delay, wait for it,
it will surely come,
it will not be late.

Habakkuk 2: 2–4

CONTENTS

An 8-page photo section appears between pages 122 and 123

ACKNOWLEDGMENTS

I would like to thank my friend, nemesis, erstwhile coauthor, and unindicted coconspirator Roderick Edward "Legs" McNeil for pointing me in the direction of this story. I would like to thank William Georgiades, Drew Hubner, and John Gillies, as always. Obviously, Bill Kelly and Howard Hunt. Thanks go to my agent, Jim Fitzgerald, and to my editor, Ella Pearce, for all her patience. To the "Ring of Fire": Tom Hubertus, Ted Paolini, John Friedlander, and Jake Ottman. To Martin Keehn, Jim Storm, Vincent Martinelli, Ross Hutkoff, Mark Connell, and Patrick Richardson for keeping me on track. Thanks to Charles Ardai for giving me a huge boost when I needed one, and to Fenton Lawless. To my mother, Jeanne Pavia. My thanks, appreciation, and undying love to my wife, Ellen Harty, for her steadfast support in the face of very trying circumstances; and to my daughter Teresa, whom I bounced on my knee while I conducted some of these interviews. And last but certainly not least, my deep gratitude to Greg Josephs, without whose help this book could quite literally not have been written.

A NOTE FROM THE AUTHOR

In an American romantic heart, it is always 1959.

This deeply mythologized past may or may not have ever existed, but the artifacts of the era live forever. Automobiles were compared to land yachts, promising a limitless and unlimited prosperity. Tailored clothing fashioned from miracle, wrinkle-resistant fabrics. White shoes. High-flying pompadours and their slicked-down, toned-down, squared-away cousins. There was money: tight money and loose money, money for mortgages and those enormous automobiles, maybe even more than one.

Gangster culture was mainstream. Hip to the lingo, guys talked out of the sides of their mouths. They knew how to handicap a horse race, how to cover the numbers on a craps table, how to bet against a point spread.

Movie stars were movie stars. Their money and their sex lives were the subjects of overheated and lascivious speculation, but these folks were bigger than the rest of us, better somehow, and we accepted that fact. The gossip rags built them up and then burned them down. The public, which underwrote the stars' obscene salaries, had to actually leave their homes in order to see movie stars, who appeared ten times life-size in ornate palaces that were dedicated to showing films.

Today's cinematic mediocrities are beamed into living rooms on a daily basis. Television, the great equalizer, the perfect delivery system of mass culture, was not in 1959 what it is now, of course. But if television was by then common-place, its untold powers were merely being hinted at. Its ulti-mate victory march forward has devoured all elements obstructing its unrelenting glare, consigning all things to the same inevitable size: Small.

Celebrity is dead. The idea of celebrity is dead. It cannot have meaning if everybody is a celebrity.

There was a sharply defined enemy in 1959: He was a Communist. It is impossible to go back in time and feel the fear that turned American palms sweaty when the Red Menace was mentioned, but paranoia or not, the entire American way of life seemed threatened. Ronald Reagan at the Berlin Wall was yet to be. The Berlin Wall was yet to be. And Ronald Reagan was plotting a postcelebrity ascendancy of his own.

The hottest issue of the 1960 American presidential cam-paign was a fight over which party was going to be tougher on Communism. Youth and good looks carried the day and the celebrity candidate won by a whisker. His charisma was so irrepressible that no one mythology could contain him. Pundits called his movie-star presidency Camelot, whose real Trinity, the novelist and spoilsport James Ellroy sneered, was "Look Good, Kick Ass, Get Laid."

Romance was in high season!

The lines were drawn, but the war was cold. Battles were not always joined with infantrymen, warships, tanks, and planes, but with tough talk, bushels of cash, and cigar butts in egg yolks. Like every war, this one needed its warriors, and they were, almost to a man, veterans of the Second World War. Their character was forged in the crucible of that great conflict. Had they been born after 1959, they might have been tempted toward ephemeral celebrity, but by that year they were bound by their own scaled-down strivings to their own modest dreams. Their belief in their country could not have been more unshakeable. America was good, and America was good for the rest of the world. Theirs was the grave romance of righteousness.

Researching a completely unrelated project, I befriended one of these cold warriors. He mentioned in passing, while discussing his career with the Federal Bureau of Investigation, his experience on a long-running security assignment. I asked him to tell me more, and he did.

While he told his soaring and sordid tale of patriotism, I drifted back to 1959 and felt the longings of my own American heart. All the things I love coalesced around a history that was not my own: unparkable land yachts and greasy hair and white shoes; gangster culture and broken-down celebrity; power on both sides of the law; the politics of my country's role in the world.

This patriot's name was Bill Kelly, and he put in the better part of thirty years with the FBI, which is a lot of work. When I finished brooding over his words, I got down to my own work. I started, naturally, with Kelly, who was extremely hospitable. He housed me and fed me. He occupies, spiritually and philosophically, the dead-center of this story.

Preliminary research turned up a notorious name from America's dirty past: E. Howard Hunt. He will live in eternal infamy in connection with the Watergate break-in (a case that Kelly was, ironically and early on, called in to investigate). I found out that the exploits of Hunt and Kelly overlapped during the period this book covers, without their ever having had direct contact, when Hunt was employed by the CIA. Now, late in life, the two had become friends who saw each other maybe once a week. Kelly reached out to Hunt on my behalf with a request for an interview. Hunt declined. I got his address from Kelly and wrote him a letter, outlining my areas of interest, and asked if he would answer some written questions. The cold warrior's heart must have thawed. That wouldn't be necessary, he said. Why not just come down and talk to me? So I did.

There were other interviews with other guys who had thrived through many decades. My accountant, in a bizarre twist of fate, was working outside the Hotel Theresa when Fidel Castro stayed there in 1960. I took this as a positive portent, but I had already determined that these stories needed to be told. I made hundreds of phone calls and spent scores of afternoons in the New York Public Library. The deeper I got involved with this project, the louder I heard the siren call of romance. This—this lean, mean bitch of a book, the one you're holding in your hands—is my response.

THE
CUBA
PROJECT

The Setup

THE LEADERS
OF MEN

On October 12, 1492, Christopher Columbus, a dubious alumnus of the University of Pavia and a Genoese sailing under the flag of Isabel and Ferdinand of Spain, struck land in what is today the Bahamas. Columbus was certain that he would arrive in the Far East by sailing west, and he would have, if the North American land mass wasn't obstructing his route. What, exactly, he hoped to accomplish remains lost to history. Of course, he hoped to find gold. And maybe he was expecting to find a primitive land that he could take over without much fuss. No one knows.[1] But Columbus sailed westward past the mutinous rumblings of a crew that wanted to toss him overboard, and though he survived to become the straw man for furious historical revisionists, their spite was centuries away.[2] Nobody could fault the ancient administrators at Pavia for erecting a bust of the Admiral in their courtyard, whether or not he had attended their institution.[3] Their man had discovered the New World.

Twelve days after making landfall, Columbus again set sail for what he thought must be Japan, and when he reached a very large island, he figured he had arrived on the Asian mainland. The Admiral was, once again, badly mistaken. He was in Cuba.[4]

Spain under Isabel and Ferdinand was the happy beneficiary of some gigantic unintended consequences. If Columbus had been hoping to open trade routes, he had found them. They just didn't go where he thought they would. The wealth of riches that subsequent voyages yielded—tobacco, sugar, cotton, aloe, and the colonies that produced these commodities—transformed the kingdom into a far-flung empire. But the would-be builders of empire would have done well to heed the words of Charles of Spain, who said in 1520, "For truly he errs who reckons that by men or riches, by unlawful canvassing or stratagems, the empire of the whole world can fall to anyone's lot. For empire comes from God alone."[5]

Charles was on to something. Whether or not God had anything to do with it is debatable, but empires are hard to maintain. The history of the next few hundred years belongs to Spain, to France, and to Holland.

Slightly tardy to the Latin American fair but by 1762 well into the game, the English wrested temporary control of the Cuban capital, Havana, from the Spanish. But the English, striving to maintain an empire of their own, were getting grief from their northern colonies. The Americans, northern genus, won independence from England in two stages, tossing off the yoke of colony for good after a second victory in the War of 1812. Seven years later, during James Monroe's presidency, the expanding United States purchased the land that would become the twenty-seventh state, then called "the Floridas," from the strapped-for-cash Spanish crown.

Emboldened by the success of their northern neighbors in the nineteenth century's first quarter, Argentina, Chile, and Venezuela fought and won wars of independence from Spain. After three-hundred-plus years of ragged glory, the empire founded for Isabel and Ferdinand was running on vapors. The governments of the newly independent Latin American nations expected the United States to recognize their sovereignty, but the cagey Monroe, not wanting to offend the Spaniard and mess up his real estate transaction, waited until the sale was final. It seems as if even before Florida was a U.S. territory, the peninsula was the site of some official double-dealing.

Serving as Monroe's secretary of state was a future president (and the son of a president), John Quincy Adams. Adams was worried that the Old World powers, especially France and Russia, might be tempted to dig deeper into the Caribbean and South America, a sphere that as far as Adams was concerned belonged to the United States. Adams argued for American dominance, and against a British proposal then on the table that was intended to keep France out of the New World.

He faced opposition within the administration, but the hawkish Adams came out on top. Monroe delivered his Doctrine to Congress on December 2, 1823, though historians have said it might as well have been called the Adams Doctrine. The United States was letting the Europeans know that the New World was closed to colonization. Further political probes would not be taken lightly. The United States would mind its own business in European wars and internal squabbles, and the Monroe government expected the Old World powers to return the favor.

The British got what they wanted, though Adams didn't care about that. France was dead in the Americas. The Monroe Doctrine stood more or less unchallenged while the United States put on economic and military muscle. Americans killed each other in the War Between the States, but managed to keep out of foreign conflicts for most of the rest of the century.

By the mid-1800s, Cuba and Puerto Rico were oddball nations, Spanish colonies in the New World. Then in 1868, Cuba launched a revolution of its own. The war dragged on for ten years with no clear-cut winner, and by the 1880s, José Martí had emerged as the patron saint of Cuban independence. Martí pioneered the century-long tradition of Cuban exile agitation from the United States, writing poems, articles, and short stories that criticized Spanish rule from his haven in New York. Nothing changed. In February 1895, the Cubans again rose against the Spanish government, and fighting broke out in the eastern part of the country. Rebel forces, with the ultranationalist Martí as their guiding spiritual force (he was killed in an early battle) scored some successes bringing the fight to the Spanish. But then Spain sent nearly a quarter-million men commanded by the ruthless General Valeriano Wyler to crush them. Wyler rounded up the rural peasantry and interned them in towns guarded by his soldiers. The filth and overcrowding brought the Cubans starvation, disease, and death.[6]

The rebels fought on, but they weren't strong enough to win. Wyler wasn't much at guerrilla war, but he made Cuba bleed; the country lost over three hundred thousand people on his watch, many dumped in limed mass graves.[7] This was the bitter fruit of Martí's revolution, a destructive war that created a power vacuum the United States was all too willing to fill. Cuba was about to trade Spanish subjugation for American proxy rule.

Back in New York, there were newspapers to sell. Joseph Pulitzer and William Randolph Hearst, respective publishers of the *New York World* and the *New York Journal*, were waging a war of their own for fortunes accumulated pennies at a time. Pulitzer and Hearst sold lust, murder, puppy dogs, pigtails, and a pom pom–waving and deep-throated hurrah for all things American. They liked a kick-ass foreign policy. There would be no appeasing Old World has-beens like

Spain, and anyway, the United States was *obliged* to help the poor, exploited Cuban. This humanitarian impulse (the press despised Wyler) together with the nationalist ravings in the so-called yellow press ignited public sympathy for expanded American influence and power in Cuba. And then the *Maine* blew up.

The battleship was sitting in Havana harbor on February 15, 1898, hardly minding her own business, but it has been said that if the *Maine* hadn't hit a mine that night, maybe Pulitzer or Hearst would have bombed her. The burning of the *Maine* was the exact act of aggression the boys needed to get themselves, their writers, and their readers howling for revenge. This was an act of despicable treachery by the swarthy and weakened Spaniard. After a two-month run-up and mounting press hysteria, the United States declared war on Spain. The marines took Guantanamo Bay, a port on the southern coast of Cuba, by late June, establishing the first American foothold of the war.[8]

Enough has been made of Theodore Roosevelt to get his face engraved on the side of a mountain, but the man was obnoxious by pretty much any measure of the word. His overweening ambition and preening self-confidence are the stuff of American legend. He served as police commissioner of the City of New York, and during the time of the Spanish-American War was enjoying a term as assistant secretary of the navy under President William McKinley. Unfortunately for Teddy, the mere sight of him was enough to make Mrs. McKinley sick. He was banned from the residential wing of the White House.[9]

But the man you hope is seated far away during a dinner party can be the same man you would follow into a hail of bullets, and Roosevelt was that guy. Despite his personal shortfalls, Teddy was a natural leader. He was much loved by the volunteer cavalry division he led, the Rough Riders, and his devoted men considered him the best soldier in the outfit.[10] He was also its best politician.

Roosevelt led the Rough Riders up not the San Juan Hill of mythology, but a nearby, shorter, and less well-defended hump the men called Kettle Hill. His troopers had been pinned down for an hour by enemy fire, getting picked off like ducks on a pond, and had no chance to shoot back.[11] There's no question that Roosevelt did lead a charge without specific orders to do so; astride his horse as his men combat-crawled a few yards at a time under withering enemy fire, the outsized New Yorker steeled his soldiers' hearts.[12]

Roosevelt returned from Cuba a hero. This was as much the result of design as it was right-place, right-time luck. Teddy had long cultivated reporters, and they didn't let him down.[13] That fall, he was elected governor of New York. Before three years had passed, he was serving as McKinley's vice president. When McKinley was killed by an assassin in 1901, he ascended to the presidency. Roosevelt was elected to a full term in 1904. With Cuban exploits contributing to his great popularity, the island nation factored into the election of the first twentieth-century American president.[14] Teddy Roosevelt would not be the last political recipient of Cuba's incidental favors.

Incorporated in 1896, the city of Miami constituted almost nothing at its founding. Florida more or less ended sixty-five miles up the coast in Palm Beach, but when Henry Flagler extended his railroad to Miami, he provided tourists with a direct link from New York City. Delirious with the booming economy of the 1920s, ordinary people incited a craze in land speculation that mirrored the overheated stock market. By 1922 the *Miami Herald* was the thickest newspaper in the country, its classified pages bursting with real estate deals.[15] Like all investment bubbles, the Florida land boom was based on nothing more than the expectation that prices would go up. And they did. For a while. In *The Fish Is Red*, Warren Hinckle and William W. Turner write that "front lots on Flagler Street [in downtown Miami were] going for $50,000 a foot. Silver-tongued real estate salesmen like William Jennings Bryan sold the blazes out of the surrounding countryside, and Miami became a boomtown where ice was rationed and sold by the cube and lumber bootlegged like liquor."[16]

By the mid-1920s, the New York banks that in part underwrote the land boom tightened credit. Stung over their losses, bankers attacked the craze as a speculative fraud. Insanely high prices scared off would-be buyers, and people who already owned land figured they better get out while they could. Eventually, only sellers remained. The real estate sharpies folded up their shops. Over the next few years, a devastating hurricane, a surreal inland tidal wave, and widespread citrus-crop destruction brought by the Mediterranean fruit fly dealt a combination of knockout punches to the state's economy.[17] The Florida land boom of the 1920s went bust for good.

In what became the Eighteenth Amendment to the Constitution, the Volstead Act of 1919 prohibited the sale, manufacture, and transportation of alcoholic beverages in the United States. While it was widely unenforced (and unenforceable), Prohibition gave rise to a gangster class in large northeastern cities. There was money to be made in booze. The fresh, illegal industry reeled in immigrants and the sons of immigrants who saw opportunity in this silly new land of plenty, young men who were literally willing to fight to make a buck. The early power in the hooch rackets belonged to the Irish and the Jews. A couple of Jewish kids from the Lower East Side of Manhattan, Meyer Lansky and Benjamin "Bugsy" Siegel, and their notorious Bug and Meyer gang, protected the turf of bootleggers like Dutch Schulz (real name: Arthur Flegenheimer), Louis Lepke, and Jake Shapiro.[18]

A wave of killings in the late Prohibition years—called the Castellammarese Wars after the Sicilian hometown of many of the combatants—changed the face of the rackets. The Mustache Petes—old-time greaseballs—brought the mayhem on themselves with hardheadedness and greed, hoarding money and power from their lieutenants. Vito Genovese and Lucky Luciano realized the only way the Mustaches were going to ease up on the reins was if they were dead, and they obliged them. The murders led to the formation of a national "commission" or board of directors made up of the heads of the twenty-four largest gangs—called families—with the real power concentrated in New York. These Sons of Italy, like Columbus before them, now had their day. Official membership was restricted to those of Italian or Sicilian descent, but one of Luciano's sharpest moves was making sure his long-time friend Meyer Lansky was squarely in his corner.

Ex–New Yorker Al Capone had by then consolidated his power in Chicago, and like many a middle-class striver in times to come, had taken to lolling away the winter in the Miami sunshine. Capone's southern drift didn't do much for Miami's national image. But he established Miami as an "open city," meaning that all organized crime elements could operate there without being bumped off by rival gangsters. Big Al figured the area was growing at a fast enough clip to create enough to share; besides, other mobsters would draw off some of the legal shrapnel that Capone attracted like a magnet.[19] And Capone wasn't stepping on any toes. The real mob power was concentrated not in Miami but in Tampa, and the boss was Santo Trafficante. Trafficante gathered the Tampa rackets unto himself, focusing on gambling in partnership with his son, Santo, Jr., and in the 1930s, the Trafficante family's tentacles stretched all the way to Havana. By the late 1950s, Santo Jr., heading a family that was greatly expanded, owned pieces of several Havana gambling joints.

During the heyday of Capone and Santo, Sr., an obscure bureaucrat, lifelong Washington, D.C., resident, and key player in our main story named John Edgar Hoover assumed control of what was called, until then, the Justice Department's Bureau of Investigation.[20] In 1935, the organization became known as the Federal Bureau of Investigation, or FBI. The criminal gangs that Hoover's G-men attacked were not Italian, Jewish, Irish, or urban: they were midwestern hayseeds on bank-robbing sprees. Coupled with the bureau's headline-grabbing investigation into the kidnapping of the Lindbergh baby, the Depression-era crime rampage of Alvin "Creepy" Karpis, Pretty Boy Floyd, and others thrust the FBI into the forefront of American tabloid culture.[21] Hoover's bureau grew in strength and wisdom, and his doggedness and absorption did more than anybody, before or since, to professionalize law enforcement in the United States.

The ascendant Americans had dumped the Spanish empire into the junkyard of history in short order: the 1898 war was over in less than six months. Three years later, the United States enacted the Platt Amendment, and it is here that America's dark obsession with Cuba—for our purposes anyway—begins for real. Encompassing seven articles, the act's main thrust reserved the right of the U.S. military to intervene in Cuba as the Americans, or the Cubans, saw fit. The idea was to maintain Cuba's newly gained "independence"; Platt also solidified the American hold on Guantanamo.[22]

José Miguel Gómez kicked off the parade of rotten politicians who would head the new Cuban republic. Gómez, who was in fact quite popular, was nicknamed "the Shark." The line in Cuba was, "the shark goes swimming but he makes a nice splash"; in other words, he knew about one hand washing the other. Entering his presidency a pauper, Gómez left it a rich man. But since the early 1900s was a time of wild prosperity on the island, Gómez was tolerated—a rising tide does indeed float all boats.[23]

He was succeeded by General Mario García Menocal, who distinguished himself from his predecessor only by being more corrupt. Unfortunately, he did not have the Shark's charm and personality. Both men plundered the national lottery (Gomez having reinstituted it, along with another great Cuban pastime, cockfighting, whose proponents cried, "Bring back the cock!").[24] Menocal outlasted a coup attempt, and he hung around until the early 1920s, when he was replaced by the equally feckless Alfredo Zayas.

Next up was Gerardo Machado, a butcher by trade. His journey into Cuban politics started in the armed forces, where he looted the military's coffers and made himself rich. As Machado swung into position for his 1924 presidential run, it was understood that he would use the spot to make himself, and his friends, even richer. So it went in Cuban politics: nobody expected any better, but then, nobody expected any worse, either. Machado was no stranger at the Havana whorehouses, and he employed a front man who operated a theater that ran porno shows. His sins were laughed off as the failings of a lovable rogue. "Chico," he'd wink while campaigning, "Come and see me," hinting that a Machado ballot would fatten the voter's own pockets. His campaign strategy worked like a charm. Machado took over in 1925.[25]

Highly impressed by Mussolini's fascist Italian state, Machado consolidated his power. He had rival political parties outlawed. One opponent was thrown to the sharks (the ocean-going variety, not the political kind). With the rubber stamp of Congress, whose members Machado bought and paid for, the president had the constitution fixed so that an executive term ran six years, rather than the four that he had been elected to serve. As the decade came to a close, Machado had the legislative body extend that term even further, until 1935 this time, without having to bother with the hassle of reelection.[26]

Machado's iron fist met violent opposition, so the president responded with more killings. One liberal newspaper editor was assassinated. With murder and mayhem spreading throughout the island, Machado's opponents called for U.S. intervention under the Platt Amendment. The United States—taking a wait and see attitude, and probably not all that thrilled with the opposition anyway—restrained itself. In August of 1931, Machado was the target of a takeover attempt led by Menocal and a colonel named Carlos Mendietta, but he crushed the uprising.[27]

After Franklin Delano Roosevelt was inaugurated in March 1933, he dispatched a special envoy to Cuba. The diplomat Sumner Welles, wrote Hugh Thomas in *Cuba*, was "more proconsul than ambassador, more politician than civil servant."[28] He tried to work out a deal between a murderous political party called ABC and some radical student groups on the one side, and the Machado regime on the other. Violence only increased.

The measly support Machado could claim came from the army. The officers knew that if Machado went down, they were going down with him, since the armed forces were keeping the president in power. Ultimately, however, Machado abandoned the presidential palace at 9:30 A.M. on August 12. A massive throng parted down the middle in utter silence as the Machado motorcade passed. But by that night, with an unpopular military figure announced, then unannounced, as Cuban president, Havana slipped into anarchy. The presidential palace was sacked and houses were laid waste. A thousand people were killed.[29]

A series of convoluted events in the days that followed, known as the Sergeants Revolution or the Revolt of the Sergeants, brought Fulgencio Batista to the forefront of Cuban politics. (He would stay there for twenty-five years, indirectly setting in motion the characters and events of the story that follows.) Batista was a sergeant stenographer and his fellow schemers were, likewise, noncommissioned officers. These NCOs had an urgent need to distinguish themselves from the commissioned officers so closely identified with the despised Machado, if only to ensure their own survival. A crisis loomed. Thirty American warships ringed the island of Cuba. A large group of Machado officers holed up at the Hotel Nacional. The United Fruit Company, an American interest also closely linked to Machado, was naturally in favor of U.S. intervention. Sumner Welles recommended as much to Roosevelt three different times. Three times Roosevelt said no.[30]

In a foreshadowing of the violence that would darken Miami decades later, expatriate Cubans loyal to former president Menocal awaited Machado, his wife, and at least one official as they made good their escape from Havana. The two sides clashed at the Miami train station, where Machado's wife and daughters were menaced by an angry mob. Police billy-clubbed the Menocal agitators and threw ten of them in jail. Their supporters followed them to the lockup, where they demonstrated for their release. The Miami police chief reacted angrily. "If they want to fight and raise hell," he said, "let them go back to Cuba."[31]

Cuban fighting Cuban would hog Miami headlines and fire American tabloid imaginations some twenty-five years down the line. This incident wasn't much more than a brawl, but the similarities are eerie. Here was the future writ small. Pitched battles between Cubans on Miami's streets would eventually capture the FBI's attention, but the men at the barricades who would push back were at this time mere lads; J. Edgar Hoover's "college boys" were still in grammar school. The as-yet-unborn FBI was mostly staffed with former sheriff's deputies and the like, scarcely a law degree among them.

For its part, under Batista, Cuba remained volatile, but economic ties between Havana and Miami got stronger. The 1930s brought commercial air travel, and Miami, with its natural geographic advantage over New York and Tampa, replaced those two cities as the main exile destination.[32] Every subsequent political upheaval in Cuba, and there were a lot of them, brought more Cubans to the Miami area.

Prohibition ended in the same year as Batista's Revolt of the Sergeants, but the death of bootlegging did nothing to shrink mob-run businesses; the rackets expanded. The protection game, old-fashioned strong-arm stuff victimizing newer immigrants, thrived in the eastern cities with their large ethnic populations. Prostitution was as popular as ever, and gangsters infiltrated the labor unions. But gambling and its inevitable offshoots—loan sharking, graft, and political corruption—pumped lifeblood into the mob. Credit Meyer Lansky for having keyed into this reality as a young hoodlum. "Gambling," he philosophized in later years, "pulls at the core of a man."[33]

Lansky's craft pulled at the cores of many men throughout the 1930s. Up and running in partnership with his old buddies Lucky Luciano, Bugsy Siegel, and others (the earliest incarnation of the American Mafia), Lansky's Piping Rock casino became a magnet for high rollers and a cash cow in Saratoga, New York. Meyer and "Jimmy Blue Eyes" Alo muscled in on the gaming business of a Hallandale, Florida, operator, then reopened it as The Farm. Meyer's fabulous Colonial Inn gave the swells fine dining and Broadway songbirds. Lansky and his partners got rich. But along the way, Lucky Luciano's luck ran out and, succumbing to an occupational hazard, he was convicted on ninety-nine counts of promoting prostitution and sentenced in 1936 to thirty to fifty years in prison.

Japan's attack on Pearl Harbor in December 1941 crippled the U.S. Pacific fleet, and the Second World War had begun badly on America's Atlantic coast, too, where German U-boats were sinking Allied merchant ships almost at will. The Nazi success implied that they had a spy in place, and the Office of Naval Intelligence, or ONI, set out to unmask him in 1942. ONI figured out that the New York waterfront, manned by Italian fishermen, might be able to supply critical intelligence on suspicious activity. Instead, it was a black hole from which no such word escaped. Meanwhile, 272 ships were sunk during the first six months of the war. Hundreds of sailors were killed. ONI reached out to Meyer Lansky, hoping he would draft the imprisoned Luciano, and through Lucky, penetrate the clannish world of the Italian waterfront. Lansky responded with a refrain that would be echoed by several gangsters in the ensuing years: "I'll help you," he said, "it's patriotism."[34] Within six months, with Lansky and Luciano in action on the navy's behalf, American intelligence agents uncovered the plot and the FBI apprehended eight Nazi spies; four in Long Island and, subsequently, four in Florida. With Lansky again leaning on a well-placed New York hood, ONI put undercover agents on the docks as long-shoremen and bar and restaurant workers, giving the navy eyes and ears on any subversive activity.[35] Luciano's war work won him release from prison. As part of his deal, on February 10, 1946, he was deported from the United States to Italy. U.S. officials were not beneath reaching into the under-world for help when they needed it, as we will see. And the overtures didn't perturb the gangsters at all. If politics makes strange bedfellows, the dirty business of war forges quirky alliances.

Throughout the 1930s, Batista, holding no specific office, operated behind the scenes as Cuba's de facto leader. His Sergeants' Revolution swallowed its first politician, Ramón Grau San Martín, when Grau was forced to resign from the presidency in 1934. Batista then ruled through a merry-go-round of puppets. Carlos Mendietta, the former colonel, lasted about a year. José Barnet and Miguel Mariano suffered similarly truncated tenures, but Federuco Laredo Brú occu-pied the president's office for four whole years. Then in 1940, with war clouds blackening Europe, an election that was widely thought to be honest was held, and Batista was chosen as president. Cuba was a staunch U.S. ally in World War II, and Cubans considered the Japanese attack to be a blow against all the nations of the Americas.

The long war caused a worldwide sugar shortage. The price went up; Cuba's economy boomed.[36] Batista was feel-ing good about himself, and when 1944 dawned and it was time to face reelection, he tapped a civilian stand-in to run in his stead. Naturally, Batista planned to exercise the lion's share of power offstage, but he overplayed the scene. His man was beaten by a revivified Ramón Grau San Martín. Alas, Grau "did more than any other single man to kill the hope of democratic practice in Cuba."[37] His administration was marked by corruption, graft, and murders committed by a hodgepodge of political gangs that were at least as vicious as their Mafia counterparts to the north.

Our story is about the realities of the postwar world, and about the Americans who shaped that world. But the war itself cemented the ideas and the opinions of the young veterans who hammered the last nails into the coffins of Nazism and empire and made it home alive. They believed in American might and American righteousness. Some of the more patriotic vets found work in Hoover's expanding FBI, and as the pieces of the postwar puzzle clicked into place, it was plain to them that Communism was the next evil that had to die. President Harry Truman endeavored to bottle up this threat and to stop its spread. The policy was called containment, and Hoover's G-men were ordered to contain it at home.

Nationalistic and anti-Yankee, Juan Perón of Argentina was a pebble in the shoe of this policy in Latin America. Not a Communist, but a military strongman and a populist, Perón reached into the influential student groups slugging it out on the streets of Havana and persuaded them to form an "anti-imperialist" league. The students were led by a fiery young man named Fidel Castro, and though the facts of his leadership, as with all things Castro, are open to debate, in Fidel's own mind, there was never any doubt.[38]

He was tall and good-looking, slick and smart. A privileged child, he was sent to a Jesuit high school and then to

Havana University. Fidel was a fierce competitor who believed that if he only tried hard enough, at baseball or political argument, he would win. He usually did.[39]

He took his cocky attitude to Bogotá, Colombia, in 1948 for the inaugural meeting of the Organization of American States (OAS). Strongly endorsed by Truman, the OAS was supposed to adopt a platform of anti-Communism; in exchange, the United States would provide aid to its poor Latin neighbors.[40] Perón, Castro, South American student delegations, and obviously the Communists stood wildly opposed to the idea. Even at this tender age, Castro understood the importance of the event and the size of the stage, and he planned to confront the United States and the OAS over their imperialist leanings. He wanted to agitate for other causes, too, such as the removal of General Rafael Trujillo from the presidency of the Dominican Republic.[41]

Castro took every chance he got to trash mouth the United States, and with a friend, distributed anti-American leaflets at a gathering of foreign bigwigs. He was collared by the Bogotá cops, but using his already sharp persuasive skills, he talked his way out of the arrest.[42] On April 7, he met with Jorge Gaitán, the Colombian politician who was leading the opposition to his country's president. Two days later, Gaitán was murdered, and the event ignited a country that was already teetering on the verge of civil war. Gaitán's alleged killer was strung up on the spot, and Bogotá disintegrated into mass chaos, five days of revolt that became known as the *Bogotazo*. The insurrection became the signal event of Castro's life up until that time. He got to see what revolution looked like up close and had the chance to take notes for the future.[43] The Bogotazo introduced young Fidel to the wider world, but it also put him in the hot, unloving spotlight of an independent service the United

States had formed just a year before: the Central Intelligence Agency.

In the Cuban election of 1948, Carlos Prío Socarrás took the presidency away from Grau; Batista, living in Florida but hardly gone, won a seat in the Cuban Senate. He promptly returned to the States. One telling note of which way the wind blew during Grau's reign: A minor bureaucrat in his department of education, fleeing his homeland after his boss got sacked, showed up in Miami with $20 million in a suitcase.[44]

Prío, though something of a democrat in the classic sense of the word, also had quite a taste for cash. In that case, he landed the right job. His favorite pastime was lounging poolside at his country estate, sipping cocktails, receiving manicures, and discussing political postings with his cronies. Smooth and charming with movie-star looks (he harbored acting aspirations), "it was difficult to dislike Prío, and difficult to take him quite seriously."[45]

Prío was an atrocious executive taking justified fire from every quarter of the political spectrum when, in 1951, Batista announced he'd be running for president (again) the following year. The scramble to form political alliances was on. No one party held sway. Rumors circulated (perhaps originating with Batista himself) that Prío planned a coup and would install himself as dictator.[46] In the end, Prío was victimized by that boogeyman of all Cuban presidents, the army, which plotted against him. That left one man standing in Cuba (though he was in fact standing in Florida) who had the weight, the name recognition, and most important, enough respect among the armed forces to lead his country once again. Reenter, amid much intrigue, Fulgencio Batista. Carlos Prío Socarrás flew to Mexico on March 13, 1952, eventually settling in Miami, for a very long goodbye.[47] He remains the last elected leader of the Cuban people.

1

BATISTA OR THE BEARD?

The son of a milkman, William Paul Kelly was born in Trenton, New Jersey, in 1926. As a high school kid, young William got out of bed at 2:30 in the morning to deliver milk and had enough of those wintry, predawn hours to last him a lifetime. He received a draft notice in 1944 and served in the navy, but by the time the Trentonian hit the high seas, World War II was winding down and Kelly completed his obligation as a ship's mailman. He was discharged in 1946, went to Georgetown University on the GI Bill, following through to Georgetown Law, where one of his professors was the future Washington power broker Edward Bennett Williams. Kelly's life had been completely untouched by Cuban politics, but he would eventually assume a spot on the front lines of America's fight against Castro.[1]

The Federal Bureau of Investigation in the 1950s was a lily-white stronghold that recruited heavily from the Catholic universities of the Northeast and the Midwest. For the young Bill Kelly, a law school grad without much interest in the law beyond the criminal code, the bureau was the perfect launching pad for a civilian career. He was sworn in November of 1952. Kelly put in his time in New York, the bureau's largest field office and a required pit stop in any FBI career, where the ambitious young agent did background checks on prospective employees of the federal government.

It should go without mentioning that the one thing a candidate for a government job could *not* have was any hint of affiliation with the Communist Party. Bill Kelly made sure those applicants were free of pink tinges. A transfer sent him to Columbia, South Carolina, where he found no Communists. Moonshiners, yes. Communists, no.

J. Edgar Hoover was a red-fighter before the FBI was even formed. Having investigated Communist doctrines and finding them wanting, Hoover, in 1919, wrote a legal brief for the U.S. Attorney General. He thought Communism stunk then, and by the 1950s, Hoover was saying "[it] is the major menace of our time. It threatens the very existence of our Western civilization."[2]

After corresponding on a near-monthly basis with Hoover about how his talents could best be deployed, FBI Special Agent Bill Kelly beefed up his existing knowledge of Spanish and immersed himself in intensive language training. He was granted a transfer to Puerto Rico.

Puerto Rico and its tropical island breezes were a welcome switch from the northeast winters Kelly remembered with no fondness from his younger days, and the posting seemed to hold out more possibilities than South Carolina. Puerto Rico was the home to many American military installations, including the naval target range at Vieques Island, and he had half the jurisdiction to himself.

"There wasn't a whole lot going on out there," Kelly said. "The VA [the veteran's club] on the eastern end of the island consisted of one black guy at a card table." Kelly was itching for some action, and although he enjoyed the weather, Puerto Rico was dullsville.[3]

Enjoying the full backing of the armed forces, during his second tilt at the presidency, Batista may have caught a break: there was no credible opposition. Meanwhile, Fidel Castro got busy fighting the government on two tracks: the daylight maneuvering of public protest and court proceedings; at night, the shadowy shiftings of conspiracy.[4] The language of Fidel's movement—yet unnamed—was, of course, leftist. The property of the "aristocracy" when the revolution came would have to be handed over to "the people." But Castro resisted collaboration with the Cuban Communist Party. He was sympathetic to their views, but had no love for their ideological rigor; he was busy distilling his own theories.[5] The party had no real power to exploit. It simply wasn't that useful. Besides, the Cuban Communists had their own power structure, and Fidel Castro was not a part of it.[6]

During 1952, Castro and his few followers published an anti-Batista hate sheet. Called *El Acusador,* the newsletter had a three-issue run: the secret police found the mimeograph machine it was printed on, smashed it, and that was the end of that. Castro also tried to broadcast anti-Batista harangues over two ham radio sets, but Batista's security apparatus seized these, too. Fidel's movement sputtered.[7]

By the summer of the next year, he was ready to replace agitation with action. His first military move, an attack on the Moncada army barracks, was shrewdly selected for its location in the rural Oriente province, far from Havana. The mostly black *guajiros* (hillbillies) broke their backs four months a year harvesting the sugar cane crop and spent the next eight out of work. Castro thought a successful attack amid the poor and pissed-off sugar workers would trigger an uprising in the province, a revolt that would spread before Batista had a chance to clamp down on it.[8] Castro's fighters would overwhelm three guards, invade the barracks compound, and capture the weapons stored there. They planned on getting away clean.[9]

The rebels set out before dawn on July 26, 1953. With 121 men (and 2 women) dressed in army uniforms that had sergeant's stripes sewn on the sleeves, they approached the guardhouses. They told the sentries, who assumed they must belong to some unknown military marching band, to "make way for the general." The soldiers waved them through, and the rebels seized their guns.[10]

Castro had stopped 150 yards short of the barracks gate. He was surprised by a two-man patrol, both armed with submachine guns. He stomped on the accelerator, but lost control of his rented Buick, hit a curb, and stalled. A sergeant now outside the compound leveled his weapon at Fidel. From positions behind their leader, the rebels opened fire. The sergeant went down. Then somebody inside the barracks set off an alarm, sounding the death knell for the Moncada attack. Over sixty rebels, not counting those killed in action, were captured, tortured, and executed.[11]

Castro was taken prisoner and under interrogation admitted everything. A Batista official issued a press release summarizing the rebel action, then stupidly let Fidel give interviews and even conduct a radio broadcast. Instead of the Cuban people turning against the rebel cause, as the officer expected, Castro was transformed in the public mind from half-baked romantic to bold leader, a man with ideas and plans.[12]

Fidel defended himself during his brief trial. The verdict was a foregone conclusion; he was found guilty and sentenced to fifteen years in prison.[13] But in an impassioned two-hour speech, the kind he was becoming famous for, Fidel told the judges and the world outside the courtroom, "History will absolve me."[14]

Throughout this same period, American interests strengthened their hold on the Cuban economy. U.S. companies controlled over three-quarters of the country's utilities, just short of half of its sugar, and ninety percent of Cuba's mineral resources.[15] But Havana was swinging. Some of the hottest music in the world was coming out of its nightclubs, there were scandalous live sex shows for those in the know, and the casinos offered more betting than any sport could reasonably crave. Meyer Lansky, always where the action was, had by then expanded operations. He joined Florida's Santo Trafficante and other American wise guys in the capital's booming gambling rackets. But Havana's gambling hells, both high and low, were running crooked games. Their operators hadn't learned the lesson Lansky built into his philosophy years before: the house doesn't need to cheat. Give the suckers fair odds and they keep on being suckers. A wide-ranging ramble by a *Saturday Evening Post* reporter of that era discovered that the only casino not rolling loaded dice was Lansky's Montmartre Club.[16]

When Meyer and his brother Jake threw open the doors of their gleaming new operation at the Hotel Nacional in 1955, Batista was, in effect, their partner. The Nacional immediately began to throw off cash. If the price of doing business was high, Meyer had dealt with that fact his whole career. "Bribes, payoffs, favors, they were meat and drink to him. In the Cuba of the 1950s," Lansky biographer Robert Lacey wrote, "that sort of corner cutting was raised to a fine art."[17]

Batista ran a greedy show. Some said his regime resembled an ongoing criminal enterprise more than it did a government.[18] Though the men avoided the vulgarity of direct cash transfers, Meyer Lansky made sure the dictator reaped a healthy chunk of *all* casino profits, to the tune of 1.28 million dollars a month.[19] Payday was Monday. One of Lansky's lieutenants would stride into the presidential palace carrying a briefcase stuffed with bills, and the loot would be allocated through Batista's chain of command, down to his despised and fearsome secret police.[20]

Havana attracted more than wise guys and swells. High rollers get all the stroking and absorb most of the perks, but the bread and butter of the casino business is the slots player clutching a bucketful of coins. Just-folks vacationing Yankees arrived in droves for holidays of sun and sin. Havana's service economy created a substantial middle class, in the capital at least, and Cuba's tourist trade boomed. In a post card from the Nacional dated 1957, from "Jane" to "Dot" in New Jersey, Jane wrote: "This is where we stayed for two days. If you want to lose your bankroll fast, this is the spot."

In 1955, an asthmatic Argentine allergist named Ernesto Guevara landed in Mexico City after some very interesting travels, and became enmeshed in the city's thriving intellectual community. Young Ernesto joined political exiles, painters, poets, and writers who had come to soak up the freewheeling atmosphere.[21] Guevara had earned a degree in medicine two years earlier, but the healing arts could not hold him. He set out to seek his fortune, and in one letter home he described himself as "100% adventurer."[22] It was adventure he would find.

Back in Cuba in the meantime, Fidel Castro's incarceration made him the most famous political prisoner in the country. The influential magazine *Bohemia* published an interview with the jailed rebel leader that gave him major national publicity. Fidel came out blazing, listing Batista's sins and detailing his own plans for revolution. Staying true to its political tin ear, the Batista government continued to underestimate Castro.[23]

Batista had held elections, as promised, in November 1954, running unopposed for president. Early the next year, he received state visits by American government officials, including Vice President Richard Nixon. Business was good. Fulgencio was feeling strong. Among the Cuban people at the same time, an amnesty campaign for the prisoners of Moncada was gaining momentum. Why spoil the party spirit with "misguided public sympathy for a few immature revolutionaries?"[24] Batista had Fidel Castro and the other *moncadalistas* released from prison on May 15, 1955. It was a profoundly arrogant and stupid move.

Castro, still bitter, vowed to pick up the fight where he left off. On June 12, out of jail and back in Havana, Fidel founded the *Movimiento 26 de Julio,* the July 26 Movement. Violence between student radicals (some who supported Castro and some who had grown indifferent to him) and Batista's security apparatus exploded, and in this overheated climate, Fidel dispatched his brother Raúl to Mexico City for safekeeping. Mutual friends introduced him to Ernesto Guevara. They saw each other almost every day. A few weeks after Raúl's arrival, Fidel came to Mexico himself and asked Guevara to join his guerilla movement. Ernesto, Guevara biographer Jon Lee Anderson wrote, "accepted on the spot."[25]

Through the early months of 1956, Castro's followers filtered into Mexico, where he organized them into cells and spread them out in various safe houses around Mexico City. The men underwent physical conditioning and arms training while Fidel worked frantically to raise money. Then, in September, he slipped into Texas from Mexico to meet with the exiled Carlos Prío Socarrás. Prío was preoccupied with his own skulduggery; one rumor had him plotting an invasion of Cuba backed by Dominican dictator Rafael Trujillo's forces. But whatever delusions Prío may have been suffering, and for reasons still obscure, Castro left his meeting with the former Cuban president with fifty thousand dollars. He spent it on an unseaworthy tub, the thirty-eight-foot yacht *Granma,* and had it overhauled.[26]

On November 25, the *Granma,* weighted down with eighty-two revolutionaries and a stack of weapons, set sail across the Gulf of Mexico bound for Oriente province in Cuba. Her voyage was a debacle. The trip was supposed to take five days; it lasted seven. The rebels got seasick. The navigator fell overboard. And when the yacht eventually did make land, she ran aground on a sandbar. The July 26ers split into two groups and wandered around a mangrove swamp for a couple of days, all the while strafed by machine gun fire that hailed down from Batista's planes.[27]

Somehow, the rebels managed to regroup. With a local peasant pointing the way, they marched in the direction of the Sierra Maestra mountain range, but were soon ambushed by Bastista's forces. The revolutionaries disintegrated in a blind panic. Men walked (or ran) in circles. Some screamed for surrender. Some froze in their tracks. Still others dropped their guns and fled. Batista's troops rounded up the stragglers, including the wounded and those who tried to surrender, and shot them.[28]

According to legend, twelve men out of the eighty-two escaped, including Fidel and Raúl Castro. Guevara was shot in the neck and abandoned his weapon, but he managed to escape as well, along with four others. Navigating by the stars, they walked east toward the mountains. But Guevara, who had now begun to be called "Che" by his Cuban comrades after Argentine custom (an American equivalent might be "buddy"), should have paid closer attention in astronomy class. It was not skill that got them into the sierra, it was dumb luck.[29]

But in the aftermath of the *Granma* disaster, Batista made another stupid mistake. His government announced that victory over the rebel interlopers had been complete. A UPI reporter wrote the story the way Batista wanted it told, and out it went over the wire, worldwide, that Fidel and Raúl Castro, along with Guevara, had been killed in action.[30]

On Christmas Eve in 1956, July 26 members or their sympathizers set off a number of bombs in Oriente. Batista hit back hard. Twenty-two government opponents were killed; two were lynched and their bodies were left hanging on the trees.[31] Batista's secret police answered every explosion in Havana by riddling an opponent (from July 26 or another group) with bullets and dumping him in the street. A bomb was then stuck in the dead man's hand. The press was alerted so that photographs could be taken; these grisly set pieces were known among *Habeneros* as "Batista's classified advertisement."[32]

There were equally horrifying "Batista Christmas presents." The week between Christmas and New Year's turned up an additional twenty-six killed in Havana; in Oriente, four more, one of whom was no more than fifteen years old. The boy had been tortured for a full day before being executed, and on January 4, his mother, amid a throng of women estimated at eight hundred strong, marched through Santiago under a banner that demanded that Batista "Stop the Murder of Our Sons."[33]

Castro's band of guerrilla fighters scored some middling successes against rural army installations. Batista's troops were not disciplined or courageous, but as if to counter this fact, the army claimed that the rebels were nothing to worry about. The pronouncement sent Castro into a rage. Desperate to disprove this misinformation, he dispatched a comrade to Havana to get out the word: Fidel was willing to talk. And on February 17, 1957, Herbert Matthews of the *New York Times* walked into the rebel camp.

A tough guy himself according to none other than Ernest Hemingway (who said the reporter was "brave as a badger"), Matthews had covered the Spanish Civil War as a young man.[34] His attachment to the left was forged by his experience in Spain; Matthews never got over the loss the fascist Nationalists handed the Republicans in that conflict. In the romance and the righteousness, the youth and the zeal of July 26, Matthews saw that death blow to socialist idealism being avenged.[35]

The effect of the Matthews series, which ran in three parts from February 24 to 26, cannot be overestimated. The July 26ers made the reporter swoon. His dispatches heralded the collapse of the old order and exposed Batista's tyranny to the *Times*'s enormous readership at home and throughout the world. Just as significant, the Matthews articles introduced these same people to Fidel Castro.

From Fidel's point of view, the interview couldn't have gone better. He arranged for a rebel soldier to interrupt the conversation with news from the "second column." If Castro's forces were split into two columns, that would have made it ten soldiers in each, since there were about twenty rebels in the mountains.[36] Fidel used the tough if sentimental Matthews as a dupe, but the most critical result of the articles was that they proved Batista, in addition to being a despot, was also a liar. Castro was far from dead: he was alive and he was fighting.

The dictator's popular support hovered near zero. He attempted to wage war on his people with a rank and file who knew they were on the wrong side of the fight. That didn't help. Batista's army vastly outnumbered Castro's forces, and they were armed to the teeth. Had they been commanded by anything resembling competent leaders, they could have defeated Castro at any time.[37]

Wayne S. Smith, a junior diplomat serving in the American embassy during Batista's last dark days, wrote, "Like the rest of the Batista regime, the army was rotten from within. Its senior officials were venal and woefully inept." Castro's rebels hit and ran in classic guerrilla style. Batista's army went after them by train, shooting out of the windows. Obviously, the lighter, quicker force had the advantage.[38]

Acceptance of Fidel Castro and his July 26 Movement were by no means a foregone conclusion. There were several groups of rebels and rebel leaders scattered throughout the country, and although the July 26 faction was the best known, its hold on the populace was shaky. The Cubans were disgusted with Batista, but if he would have gotten out of the way and allowed a transitional government to take over, it would most likely have gained support. Castro and his ragtag fighters would have been a stranded redundancy in the Sierra Maestra, with no real reason for being.[39]

Instead, the violence was ramped up. Manuel Ray was the head of a Castro sabotage unit meant to blow up electric plants and similar installations, but his efforts, like most of the other maneuvers of the rebels, accomplished almost nothing. When Ray, acting on behalf of Castro, called a general strike in May, it met with a half-hearted response. Those who did rally to the call of July 26 merely identified themselves with the rebel cause and made it easier for Batista to kill them.[40]

Emboldened, Batista went on the offensive. He launched what could have been, with competent commanders directing motivated troops, the coup de grace. But by August his miserable army was on the run again. Castro chose to counterattack, and as a result his July 26ers came to the forefront of the opposition groups.[41]

John Foster Dulles was the Republican Party's foreign policy maven, author of the U.S. peace treaty with Japan signed in 1951,[42] and a man who, in a losing Senate bid, baited the eventual winner by saying the other guy would sweep the red vote.[43] He hated Communists, and he was also Dwight Eisenhower's secretary of state. Dulles was deeply religious, a bit of a bluenose, and had become incredibly wealthy practicing corporate law. In Dulles's view, the whole world wanted to be like America. He saw Communism, Stephen Ambrose wrote in *Rise to Globalism*, as an "unmitigated evil imposed by a conspiracy on helpless people; there could be no permanent reconciliation with Communism because 'this is an irreconcilable conflict.'"[44]

Dulles's State Department fumbled and stumbled over Cuban policy. Castro clearly represented the populist element; in other words, compared to the average American politico, he was a leftist, although nobody knew how far. But cold warriors like Dulles opposed left-influenced governments, period, and they backed every stripe of right-wing bully in Latin America. Besides Batista, there was Gustavo Rojas Pinilla in Colombia, the Somoza dynasty in Nicaragua, and Batista's counterpart in the Dominican Republic, Rafael Trujillo.[45] American officials thought they were shoring up the barricades against Communism.

Castro, preaching the populist gospel of the redistribution of wealth, and with his undisguised contempt for Yankee imperialism, found no friends among American hard-liners. But whatever support Batista clung to under Ike's administration was fading fast. Now, the State Department was stuck. Nobody could defend Batista, but they were unprepared for Castro. Officials seemed to be hoping for the best and tried to promote Castro as an agrarian reformer. They sought some "middle way" to squeeze out Batista and slip some moderate into the breach. But the footpath to this middle ground was land-mined by Ambassador Earl E. T. Smith, a patrician Republican and Eisenhower campaign donor who was laboring under the delusion that there was room for Batista elements in a post-Batista Cuba. Leveler heads at State knew the Cubans would never sit still for that, but Smith stuck to his guns, and the middle way evaporated.[46]

Batista was pressured, from within and without, to promise "honest" elections, and the only person keeping a straight face, it seems, was Ambassador Smith. The elections were ultimately held in the autumn of 1958, and the contest was won, in a shocker, by a Batista lap dog. The poll, which most Cubans didn't bother participating in, was a free-for-all that stood out for its stuffed ballot boxes and its dead men disinterring themselves for this once-in-a-deathtime opportunity to cast their lots with the dictator's stooge.

Of Ambassador Smith, Wayne Smith wrote, "His real hope, despite his references to a national coalition, was to keep the Batista government, or some variant of it, in power. He had, after all, become friendly with the dictator and obviously saw him as a bulwark against Communism. In fact, Batista was exactly the opposite: it was Batista who brought about the conditions that opened the door to radical solutions."[47]

The rigged election was the last straw, even for Ambassador Smith. On the night of December 9, 1958, a Republican businessman was dispatched on the quiet by President Eisenhower to urge Batista to leave the country. He refused. Then on December 17, Ambassador Smith personally carried Washington's instructions to Batista: Get out.[48]

American policymakers weren't the only ones shoved to the sidelines while the Castro revolution played out. A pipe bomb or two set off in the right spots in Havana had the same effect as a hundred bombs on the gambling business.[49] Sensible people stayed home. Though rebel activity had a chilling effect on their profits, the casino operators never saw Castro coming, and if they did, they must have had faith that Batista's forces would prevail.

The South Florida and Havana mobster Santo Trafficante, Jr. said, "Nobody ever dreamt that [Castro] would come to power at that time." The newspapers, at least the ones that Santo was reading, dismissed Castro as nothing more than a bandit.[50]

Had Trafficante and Meyer Lansky listened to other sources, they would have known that Castro's first order of business was to scrub the country clean of American mob influence. "Fidel Castro had already proclaimed from the mountains," Robert Lacey wrote, "his intention of sluicing away the Yankee gangsters who ran the casinos of Havana. 'We are not only disposed to deport the gangsters, but to shoot them.'" Gambling in his country represented, for Fidel, all that was sick about the capitalist system. And America used the sleazy industry to spread its disease to Cuba. Corruption, repression, payoffs, and bribes, they all came together on the gaming floors of the Havana hotels.[51]

Batista clung to power after it was made clear, even to him, that Washington had washed its hands of his government. And despite the threat of violence and lingering uncertainty, during the week between Christmas and New Year's the Havana casinos were doing their usual holiday business.

One Capri hotel employee hit the Havana scene with his own brand of glamour. The actor George Raft was noted for the authenticity he brought to the screen, especially in Howard Hawk's 1933 *Scarface*, where he played Paul Muni's star-crossed, coin-flipping sidekick. Raft wasn't imitating anybody; guys on the street were trying to imitate the actor. The pinstripes, the grace (Raft was a dancer who once worked with Rudolf Valentino), the stiff-lipped delivery—George Raft, Hollywood tough guy, showed the real-life gangsters how it was done.

Sadly for Georgie, by late 1958 he was no longer a star; he was a footnote, another actor hustling to make a buck. Fortune's wheel had turned but Raft's lifestyle had stayed the same, and the man had an unquenchable thirst for cash. "Sometimes I wouldn't bother getting out of bed," Raft said of those days, "because as soon as my feet hit the carpet I needed a grand."[52]

This wasn't the first taste of hard times, relatively speaking, for the former star. He had labored previously as an "entertainment consultant" at Benjamin "Bugsy" Siegel's reconstituted Flamingo Hotel in Las Vegas (reconstituted without the Bug, who had been murdered). He had tried to buy into a new ownership structure headed up by a Beverly Hills businessman, but Raft was denied by Nevada authorities, who cited his long history with wise guys like Siegel. The Nevada Gaming Commission later reversed itself and okayed the deal, but Raft was forced to sell soon after as his money woes—and his high-octane lifestyle—persisted.[53]

Then in the spring of 1958, Jerry Brooks, an old pal, called to offer Raft the job of entertainment director at the Capri hotel and casino in Havana. Brooks was managing the joint. After that gig ended, Raft scored a part in Billy Wilder's *Some Like It Hot*, set partially, as it happened, in Miami. The movie wrapped and the actor went back to Los Angeles, maybe to brood about how much money he didn't have, but otherwise not too busy. The phone eventually rang and it was Brooks again on the other end of the line. He was hoping that Raft could show up for Christmas, Brooks's busy week, and Georgie came through for his friend. He arrived at the Capri on December 24, 1958.

George Raft wasn't the only Hollywood has-been haunting Havana at the time of the revolution. Errol Flynn had long used the island as a private hideout. The Tasmanian-born leading man played a number of swashbuckling roles, as a pirate in *Captain Blood* and the title part in an early iteration of Robin Hood. Flynn's reputation was dirtied by his taste for underage girls (he beat a statutory rape charge), and he loved Cuba because he could act whatever way he wanted—usually badly—and not have to worry about Hollywood gossipmongers bloodhounding his tracks.[54] Miraculously, the washed-up drunk managed to land himself a position with William Randolph Hearst's *New York Journal-American* as a war correspondent. He claimed to have spent time with the July 26ers, but whether or not he got close to the fighting is a matter of some dispute.[55] Wayne Smith, the American diplomat who witnessed firsthand the fall of Havana, casts some doubt on Flynn's fanciful accounts. Smith and his wife liked to hang out at the Bodeguita del Medio, a joint that was always jumping, even in those dying days of the Batista regime, and Flynn had a corner table with his name on it. If Flynn witnessed any combat, his trip to the mountains was a quick one, "for the corner table," Smith said, "was rarely unoccupied."[56]

Maybe the aged lothario saw some action, maybe not, but his dispatches back to the states portrayed Fidel in a warm pink light.[57] And in any event, Flynn's journalistic foray served its purpose: self-promotion. People gobbled it up. And this half-cocked adventure fit Flynn's idealized version of himself. With his glory days decades behind him, he was a real life Robin Hood without the tights. But instead of matching wits with the Sheriff of Nottingham, he was aiding the pitched battle against the evil despot Batista.[58]

"By the end of December," Wayne Smith wrote, "bets were being taken as to when the dictator would flee."[59] It would be wrong to say Castro's rebels won in any military sense; Batista's troops quit. The effect was the same. Castro's men took the town of Palma Soriano, near Santiago, where Errol Flynn claimed to be, and on December 31 rebel forces were also in Havana.[60] "Everything was in turmoil," Santo Trafficante said. "There was people all over the streets, breaking into homes, there was complete enmity and the only thing at that time was to try and stay alive."[61]

George Raft was completely oblivious to all the noise. On New Year's Eve 1958, after shaking the requisite hands and quaffing the requisite bubbly, Raft had decided to call it a night's work at the Capri. He went back to his suite and his "special silk sheets" and to the Cuban beauty who was keeping them toasty. "Suddenly," Raft recalled, "machine gun fire!" Prying himself away from his bedmate, Raft called the front desk. "Mr. Raft," the operator said, "the revolution is here. Fidel Castro has taken over everything. He's in Havana. Batista has left."[62]

"The rest of the country," said Smith, "woke up the next morning to face not only a hangover, but an uncertain future."[63]

2

THE REVOLUTION HAS NOTHING TO ASK FOR

In the immediate aftermath of Batista's midnight flight to the Dominican Republic, where he sought refuge with Trujillo, Havana's exhilaration dissolved to violence. Responding to the rebel rhetoric about corrupt Yankee gangsters, delirious mobs attacked the casinos. They used sledge-hammers to smash slot machines, gaming tables, and parking meters. Bands of armed thugs roamed the streets of the capital, taking what they wanted where they could.[1]

After his alarming connection with the Capri's switchboard operator, George Raft beat it downstairs to the lobby. Those first hours of New Year's Day found a vengeful mob at the hotel's doorstep.[2] Legend has it that the snarling Raft stood at the entrance of the gaming floor, his arms outstretched, his teeth gritted, and hissed, "Yer not coming in my casino." The mob, evidently uncertain if they were in a movie or if this was actually happening in three dimensions, set off elsewhere.[3] In Raft's humble and more believable version of the event, he was terrified. The bar got shot up and Raft, wearing a pair of slippers that it cost a grand to hit the carpet in, got on top of a table and told everybody "For Chrisssake, calm down." To his tremendous relief, it worked.[4]

A couple of days later, when genuine rebel soldiers, as opposed to opportunistic criminals, arrived at the Capri, almost two hundred of them bivouacked on the fourth and

fifth floors as "guests of the house," and there were no problems. In the meantime, Raft tried desperately to contact anyone with an iota of authority. He put in calls to Ambassador
Smith and J. Edgar Hoover, but was unable to get a response.
Stuck in the hotel with all the guests from New Year's Eve
and the rebel fighters upstairs, Raft was forced to stay.[5] A
credulous dispatch filed not from Havana but from Hollywood by gossip columnist Louella Parsons reported that
Raft, long a favorite of Cuban cineastes, was being "protected" by Castro partisans, and in fact, had been made an
"honorary lieutenant."[6]

Finally, two weeks after he arrived to meet and greet during the bustling Havana holidays, Raft was escorted to the
airport by a pair of rebel soldiers. Once he got there, the
movie tough guy was surrounded by four armed men,
pulled off the boarding ramp, and detained. He was grilled,
and somebody stole his hat.[7] The linings of his suitcase were
sliced open.[8] "Then this one guy searched me and took all the
money I had on me, twenty-eight hundred in cash,"' Raft
said. "[They] slammed me up against the wall. They stepped
back like they were a firing squad and these three goons
pointed guns at my head. Then," Raft went on, "came the
final insult. This captain, with a big shiteating grin on his
face, comes up to me with one of my publicity photos. He
holds it out with a pen and asks for my autograph."[9]

Rushed by reporters upon his return, Raft was photographed with the stub of a cigarette dangling from his lips,
his tie deliberately undone. In this frozen moment, it is impossible not to love the thin-haired, sixty-three-year-old former movie star. True to his street beginnings and probably
uneager to stir up further controversy, Georgie stayed mum
about the roughing up he got from Cuban authorities. Raft
was also characteristically cool when it came to talking about

his employers. "A whole bunch of people own the casino," he said breezily, and as to when or if the gambling spots would reopen, Georgie just couldn't say.[10]

On the other hand, Errol Flynn, in a photograph from the same week, resembled a version of himself that might have appeared at Madame Tussaud's Wax Museum. Draped with a scarf he said Castro gave him, his ridiculous pencil moustache clipped tight, Flynn regaled scribes with stories of his exploits with the rebels. He played down a minor wound he said he suffered while accompanying Castro forces on a raid, a tidbit on the UPI wire that found its way into an FBI file on the actor.[11]

Unlike Raft, Flynn couldn't keep his mouth shut about politics. Perhaps Georgie, knowing which side his bread was buttered on—the gangster side—wanted to distance himself from the element. Flynn had no such ties. He was a great admirer of Castro, said he had known him for eight years, and took the assignment from the *Journal-American* because he "wanted to see what made an idealist tick."[12] A wire service story had Flynn holding forth on Castro's political orientation, saying he was sure that Fidel was not a Communist. Maybe a few of the July 26ers were red, the thespian opined, but the Communist sympathizers had no interest in any role in a postrevolution government.[13]

Miami International Airport on the first few days after New Year's had a chaotic flavor of its own. Some of Castro's stateside partisans had gotten word that the Havana police chief was at the Pan Am terminal, and a mob of exile Cubans, including those who had fled Batista repression but had no special love for the July 26 Movement, set after the lawman in search of righteous vengeance. Then came the word that some Batista cops were still clearing customs. The throng would not be swayed. A small group, led by Miami police, was allowed inside. No Batista loyalists were found. But a brawl did erupt between a pair of Cubans, and they were pulled apart by a third party whose good deed did not go unpunished. The peacemaker got punched out, too, shades of the violence that was to grip the exile population in the months to come.[14]

Castroites planned a victory parade through the downtown Miami business district, but the police chief wisely squashed their plans; with remnants of the despised regime landing and old animosities ignited, the Cuban neighborhood around the Calle Ocho could have been an even uglier scene than Havana on New Year's Day.[15]

The Capri Hotel's switchboard operator, understandably excited, was mistaken on the specifics. Castro's men were in Havana, but Fidel's own trip to the capital took him over a week. He walked. On this bipedal public relations tour, Castro talked to every media representative that stuck a microphone on front of him, and there was no shortage of offers. "He had a walkathon, you would call it, from the mountains to Havana," Trafficante recalled, "and they kept interviewing him and he kept saying the casinos would close."[16]

Preliminary reports to the states had Meyer Lansky and his gangster pals hauling ass out of Havana on Batista's coattails. Santo Trafficante, by now wanted for questioning in the unsolved rub-out of Brooklyn Mafioso and Murder Inc. founder Albert Anastasia, was alleged to be on one of three chartered planes bound for New York. New York Police Department detectives dispatched a unit to collar them at Idlewild (now JFK) airport. They found only relieved tourists, and the story went that the racketeers got word of the NYPD's welcome wagon and ordered their aircraft diverted to Jacksonville, where they presumably disembarked for points west.[17]

This sequence of events doesn't add up. The casino operators had already survived two upheavals in Cuban government and their experience would have led them to persevere. And with an estimated two million dollars a night at stake, Lansky and the others weren't about to cut and run.

Meyer Lansky, for his part, stuck around Havana until January 7, and then, after a brief trip to the states, flew back to Cuba. By the end of the month, he was doing the best he could, as were his associates, to iron out a working deal with the new Cuban government.

The gambling industry and the men who ran it were marooned in a Castro-imposed limbo for weeks after the revolution took hold, their future bleak. Castro kept up the party line about Yankee gangsters until he was forced to confront the realities of actually *running* a government instead of being in charismatic opposition to one. During the last week of that first month of his revolution, thousands of casino employees who had been tossed out of their jobs took to the streets in a massive protest.[18]

With the revolution's credibility among the working class at stake, the new government was obliged to reconsider. After lecturing the racketeers about the way they made a living, a Castro official granted them a sixty-day license to operate, and the Havana casinos reopened during the last week of February 1959. The official warned that the permits would not be renewed for gangsters, but the hoods hoped they could put forth a new crew of front men that might pass the revolutionary litmus test. Lansky, Trafficante, and the others were harassed into reopening their gaming operations so casino workers could catch up on the back pay they missed when Castro shut them down. There was an air of inevitability regarding the mob element. Castro needed these men for the short term. One sharpie said, "Only gamblers can run casinos—you can't have a priest or a garage mechanic."[19]

Santo Trafficante for a time was effectively in the direct employ of the revolutionary government. Accused of being a Batista collaborator, which was true, Santo was subject to constant bullying. Castro thugs would raid his apartment looking for cash, then drag him off to the woods for questioning. "Most of them were fifteen, sixteen, seventeen years old," he said. "They had weapons. It was a bad time to be there."[20]

The initial United States reaction to Castro was cautious but favorable. Castro installed a civilian, Manuel Urrutia, as provisional president, who set out immediately to repeal martial law and establish civilian authority. A V. I. Lenin look-alike right down to the goatee, Urrutia promised the Cuban people a new constitution and stacked his cabinet with a collection of anti-Batista elements, not all of whom were armed rebels. The *Miami Herald,* in an editorial dated January 7, 1959, figured that these were all good things—so long as "Cuba can return to the pursuits of wealth and happiness with its business structure unimpaired and the rights of foreigners protected." The biggest question mark of all, the writer said, was Fidel Castro himself, and asked, in an encouraging tone, "Is this Cuba's main chance?"[21]

Two days later, the *Herald*'s editorial page took up the subject again. Quoting a State Department press release, which stated that the Eisenhower administration was satisfied with "the assurances given by the new government of Cuba of its intentions to comply with [its] international obligations," the paper took a few sideswipes at foreign diplomats for being so unprepared for Castro's ascension. The writer wondered aloud about the loyalty of Batista's supposedly superior soldiers, going so far as to ask if his forces ever fought in any "real battles," but the overall tone of the piece was hopeful. Still, the editorialist reminded the emerging government of its responsibility to establish a "democratic constitution" and "free elections . . . at the earliest possible opportunity."[22]

Castro called his revolution "the purest and gentlest in the world," and seemed intent on letting civilians run the new government.[23] He joined his provisional president in calling for an end to censorship.[24] This was exactly what American officials hoped to hear. Indeed, "the general public in the United States welcomed Castro," historian Stephen Ambrose commented, "casting him in a romantic mold and applauding his democratic reforms."[25]

The more parochially inclined, like *Herald* columnist Jack Kofoed, were worried about where the gambling industry was headed now that Havana's casino business seemed doomed. Their fears were fueled by a concurrent drive to bring legalized gaming to Miami Beach, but failing that, a return to the good old bad old days. "Illegal casinos might be winked at, as they were in the past," Kofoed fretted. As far as the columnist was concerned, Batista's ouster and Castro's subsequent casino ban were an invitation to return to the wide-open times of the 1930s and '40s. Back then, police and elected officials held hands with the underworld element that thrived in the corrupt environment, stuffing each other's pockets with cash.[26]

The American public had other reasons to look askance. In the first weeks after the dictator was run out of Cuba, Castroites turned on Batista officials with a bloodlust reminiscent of the French Revolution. The hacks of the Cuban ancien régime were put to death by the dozens; the number killed grew into the hundreds. Any high-ranking officer of the

Batista army luckless enough to remain in Cuba after the Castro takeover was a dead man walking. One major, convicted of "genocide" in the first of Havana's show trials, was granted a new hearing in late February. The verdict didn't change, and neither did the sentence: death by firing squad. The officer's execution brought the unofficial number to 316. His last words were, "I forgive you boys, and I hope you forgive me."[27]

But most high-ranking Batista officials, civilian and military, had the connections and the sense to get themselves out of the country before these "revolutionary tribunals" began. That left ordinary soldiers as the only remaining targets. They were not spared.

When Castro didn't like the verdict handed down by his own revolutionary court, he simply overrode it. In March, some pilots, gunners, and even mechanics who had served in Batista's air force were acquitted of "genocide, murder, and homicide." Castro appointed a review court that delivered a decision to his liking, and the defendants were convicted. The pilots were sentenced to thirty years' hard labor; the others received less stringent punishment, and two men were actually found not guilty. The Havana, Santiago, and National Bar Associations lodged a protest. One lawyer said that Castro, by taking justice into his own hands, threatened to become "a new Napoleon in the Caribbean." In the meantime, the rifles of the Castro firing squads stayed hot. Thirty more "convicts" were gunned down and the total swelled to 392 by the second week of March.[28]

If Castro threatened to become Cuba's Napoleon, Che Guevara would have to be considered its Robespierre. He was more than up to the executioner's job. Back in '57, when a traitor was discovered among the July 26ers, Guevara shot the man in the head and then for good measure stole his watch.[29] Now, in the name of Marxist purity, this brave hero of the revolution signed the death warrants of hundreds of men from his perch at La Cabana fortress. Trials of sometimes five hours in length ended in guilty verdicts, the convict marched to *la pared*, the wall.[30]

American congressmen called these proceedings what they were: a blood bath. To negate the bad publicity, Castro invited foreign reporters to cover the trials he was holding at Havana's Sports Stadium, but the journalists were shocked. Not Herb Matthews of the *New York Times*. He stayed on board. Justifying the circuslike "legal" proceedings from what he called the Cuban perspective, he wrote up an apologetic editorial. His boss killed it.[31]

The United States government, the American public, and the media were torn over whether Castro was a Communist. He certainly talked like one. "The goal of his romanticism," *Newsweek* opined in April 1959, "has a Communist ring to it—a country in which there are no rich and no poor, a country in which everyone is a member of the middle class." Appealing to a populist base, Fidel promised that all farmers would own their land, which was great for the farmers but drove investment capital into hiding. His scheme to redistribute income by reducing the rents of the cities' poorest residents killed the construction industry (and the salaries of construction *workers*) and stopped the real estate market dead in its tracks.[32]

On the intelligence level, there was uncertainty. Castro was a nationalist and a reformer in a country in desperate need of reform, but a democrat? Havana diplomats could find no official link to Castro and Cuban communism, and "The CIA, for the most part, seemed to agree," according to historian David Halberstam. Testifying before a Senate Committee, the Central Intelligence Agency's deputy director,

General Charles Cabell, reported "that Castro does not consider himself to be a Communist."[33]

"For the most part" and "seemed" reflect the hedging attitude of intelligence experts, but privately, CIA chief Allen Dulles told President Eisenhower that "Communists and other extreme radicals appear to have penetrated the Castro movement." Dulles advised him that the Communists would most likely play a role in Castro's government.[34]

As for Castro himself, the penny was still in the air. Despite, or maybe because of, this degree of uncertainty, relations between Cuba and the United States during those first critical months of 1959 were almost cordial. The State Department, playing catch up, did what it could to demonstrate a willingness to work with the new government. State was cold-shouldered at every turn. But even if Castro were to have reached for whatever olive branches the department might have been holding out for him, as Wayne Smith noted, this wouldn't have served Castro's larger purpose—to play a starring role not just in Cuba, maybe not even just in Latin America, but on the world stage.[35]

Fidel's curtain call was coming.

During the time of the Cuban revolution, the population of the city of Miami was overwhelmingly white. The story of Cuban immigration to South Florida for political and economic reasons is as old as the city itself, but the number remained modest, constituting a small enclave. Many of them were refugees from Batista tyranny. But when the dictator fled, his henchmen were right behind him, if they could make it, and more military officials and shadowy representatives of Batista repression were landing in Miami every day. Among the first civilians to leave their homeland were Cuba's social and industrial elite, and the stories are numerous of *Habaneras* touching American shores draped in diamonds and furs, their husbands dressed in silk and carrying briefcases full of cash. Cubans opposed to the Castro movement but in no sense Batista partisans constituted their own subset of the growing exile community. Before long, this wave included doctors and lawyers, members of Cuba's professional and middle classes. The urban poor and the rural peasantry followed them.

Batista victims, Batista hacks, Castro partisans (many lived in Miami *before* the revolution), and Castro haters combined to form a roiling exile mix. Those without a specific political orientation or existing party loyalty, i.e., Cubans who had lived in the States for a while already, were evenly divided on the topic of Fidel Castro.

Contradictory evidence within American government offices continued to mount. The State Department was obliged to take a wait-and-see approach toward the new government in Cuba. But as far as J. Edgar Hoover's Federal Bureau of Investigation was concerned, Fidel Castro was the worst possible thing that could have happened to Cuba. The architect of FBI's opinion on Castro was George Evan Davis, the most senior street agent in the Miami field office, and there wasn't much question in Davis's mind: Castro was red. A dividing line seems to be the *Granma* incident, after which the FBI warned State to keep an eye on Fidel Castro as a possible Communist threat. Davis's opinion may have been based on Fidel's association with Che Guevara and was most likely influenced by contacts within the CIA, which had been dogging Che since his travels through Central America and Mexico.[36]

Davis's knowledge and experience exerted a good deal of influence over the Miami Special Agent in Charge (or SAC), Lee Teague. Part American Indian, this native Oklahoman and old-time Hooverite inspired tremendous respect among his agents and was nearing retirement by this time. A great favorite of Hoover's (although he continued to pronounce the man's name "Tag"), Teague took Davis's information to bureau headquarters in Washington. The State Department was then duly informed, but if anybody there took the Davis opinion seriously, it didn't have much bearing on subsequent policy. Teague had another headache: with a swelling number of Cubans arriving in Miami on a near-daily basis, he had his hands full, and he knew he needed help.

Back in San Juan, a bored Bill Kelly got an expedite transfer to Miami: pack and go. The agent and his wife, Virginia, arrived in Miami on March 3, 1959, where Special Agent Howard Albaugh informed him that he was putting him to work on an internal security team. He assigned Kelly to the Cuban Squad, joining Davis, Bob Dwyer, and others.[37]

A few months later, another San Juan agent got his own transfer orders. A combat infantryman in World War II, Bill Holloman fought in the Battle of the Bulge. He attended the University of Mississippi on the GI Bill, started on the Ole Miss football team, and after graduation and a year in California, landed a job with the FBI. Holloman had a choice to make. He could have gone to a desk job in Washington, D.C., to Cuba as a legal attaché, or to Miami. By this time the head of a young family, Holloman opted for Miami. Kelly picked him up at the airport.

One of Holloman's first responsibilities was to debrief Cuban exiles. The assignment allowed him to hear firsthand accounts of the show trials and mass executions that the Castro government was conducting in the name of revolution. Some of the Cubans he interviewed were ranking officers in the Batista army.[38] But not every Cuban émigré was a sadistic

Batista stooge. Many were simply anti-Communist, but to be anti-Communist in Cuba in 1959 was to be counterrevolutionary, and to be counterrevolutionary was to earn a ticket to La Cabana fortress and a date with the executioner.[39]

Outside of what the men were picking up from their debriefings, Miami FBI had a dearth of human intelligence. They needed informants. Kelly got to work on wiretaps, and he devoted his first months in Miami to listening in on other people's phone calls. Although Kelly's Spanish was passable, he was not completely bilingual, and the other non-Spanish-speaking agents' efforts were hindered by the availability of only one full-time translator.

Howard Albaugh expanded his Cuban team. With Holloman and others transferring in, agents split into two groups. George Davis supervised agents charged with developing intelligence on anti-Castro partisans. Kelly and Holloman birddogged pro-Castro people, and Albaugh, the overall squad supervisor, was also in charge of their pro-Castro subsection. In 1959, the Cuban Squad totaled ten agents. Within the year, that number would double. The agents became known to one another as the Tamale Squad.[40] The nickname sounded slightly contemptuous if vaguely Spanish, as tamales are more closely associated with Mexico than with Cuba. And so, with more than half the crew unfamiliar with the language, with no informants, and with no real idea of what was coming their way, Bill Kelly, Bill Holloman, Bob Dwyer, and the others set out to keep the nation safe from the Communist menace.

"Our job on the pro-Castro squad was to suppress the violent activities against the anti-Castro people," Kelly said. The Cuban expatriates "were fighting each other with sticks, stones, anything they could get their hands on."[41] But local cops break up street brawls. The Federal Bureau of

Investigation, mandated to investigate infractions against federal statutes, had a deeper, more sophisticated problem on its hands: preventing possible violations of the Neutrality Act. The FBI would have been operating in the spirit and letter of the law as articulated in the act's Section 1 (a): "it shall thereafter be unlawful to export, or attempt to export, or cause to be exported, any ammunition or implements of war from any place in the United States to any belligerent state," or in the case of Cuba, to bellicose parties. One of those belligerent factions was right here at home. Toward the end of the year, FBI Miami pulled the plug on its wiretaps, and the Tamale Squad hit the street.

A lthough not invited as an official guest of state, Castro visited the United States in April of 1959, flashing the right signals and making the right noises for a press corps that seemed determined to love him. Younger Americans treated him like a rock star. Whenever kids spotted Castro or a bearded member of his entourage, they shrieked with excitement. Even the State Department with its ongoing skepticism toward Castro and Castroism had one official admitting, "The guy makes a good showing. He handled himself well."[42]

A few nagging questions did remain. There were those untidy reports of executions to deal with, and Fidel slipped a bit when the subject of elections came up, referring to them as maybe four years down the line. He was forced into a weak explanation. "I know it is hard to believe, but the people of Cuba do not want elections now." The Havana newsman who accompanied Fidel north concurred.[43]

Fewer in number but more shrill in tone, the voices of dissent were determined to be heard. Cuban journalist Salvador Diaz-Verson contended that judging from what he saw in

Washington, Cuba had "two governments—one for appearances outside the country and one for rule inside."

Diaz-Verson charged that the man running what
amounted to a "cominform," or ruling council of Communists, was none other than Che Guevara. Interestingly, the
veteran Latin red-fighter said he didn't believe that Castro
was interested in the philosophy of Communism, but called
him a "Communist tool."[44]

Diaz-Verson was investigating Cuban Communism when
the second Batista regime took power in 1952, but he was
useful enough to the dictator, for a short time anyway, to re-
tain a position in Batista's government. He uncovered a spy
cell at the Soviet embassy in Havana which led the Batista
government to break off diplomatic relations with Moscow.[45]

Diaz-Verson kept files on Communists in Cuba and
throughout Latin America at the offices of his magazine, *Oc-
cidente*. On January 24, 1959, his offices were trashed and the
files stolen. Two days later his car was strafed with gunfire,
and, taking a hint, the editor got himself and his family out of
the country. Many of the names that he'd been tracking for
years popped up anew as members of the Castro government; Raúl Castro for one, Che Guevara obviously, David
Salvador, who was Castro's labor secretary, and Carlos Franqui, editor of the July 26 organ, *Revolución*. All had lengthy, if
not lifelong, Communist ties.[46]

The small bit of negative press that Castro received didn't
hinder his triumphant arrival in New York, and neither did
intelligence indicating there was a plot to murder Fidel when
he arrived in the Big City of Dreams. He acted like any other
tourist. He visited the Empire State Building. He shook
hands. He flirted with the girls.

Castro aides tipped New York cops on the assassination
plan, but when the would-be hit man and supposed associate

of Meyer Lansky was contacted in Las Vegas, he said this was the first he was hearing about it. Another story had five brothers of Italian American extraction heading north from Philadelphia to send Fidel into the big nowhere, but when Philly cops ran down the lead, they found all five brothers hard at work at their respective places of employment.[47]

Fidel made a big show of his indifference to the persistent rumors that his enemies had found the time and the place to take him out. The New York Police Department was forced to take matters a bit more seriously. On the evening of April 24, Castro was scheduled to address a throng of well-wishers and supporters in Central Park. Thirty-five thousand turned out to hear him, and NYPD detached a thousand-man security team including patrolmen, detectives, mounted and motorcycle cops to protect him. Fidel wanted to deliver an uninterrupted six-hour monologue. The cops haggled it down to two.

Fidel's keynote began amid wild enthusiasm, and The Beard was so caught up in the moment, it appeared that he was poised to bound down from the stage, the better to be among his people. Sharp looks from a phalanx of cops dissuaded him. Absorbing the shouted *Vivas!* rumbling into the night air, Fidel told the crowd, "I have not come here to ask for anything. The Revolution has nothing to ask for."[48]

Two of those thousand cops, Detective Frank Weber and Patrolman Walter Merlino, were maintaining a post near the band-shell-covered stage. Weber noticed one man getting too close to the back of the band-shell and told him to move.[49] Their suspicions alerted, Weber grabbed the guy and Merlino frisked him. Out fell an eleven-inch section of aluminum cut from a vacuum cleaner handle. One end of the tube was plugged with plaster, and the other end was fitted with Scotch tape, a cigarette, and some wooden matches. In between, the aluminum was stuffed with a mixture of sulphur and zinc.[50] The man's name was John Gregory Feller, an Air Force veteran from near Boston, and a riveter by trade though he wasn't working at the time. He was staying in a furnished room in the East 20s. Confronted with the innards of his vacuum cleaner handle, he admitted that yeah, it was a bomb. But just a little one. It wasn't going to do any damage.[51]

The cops wondered whether it was set to go off, but Feller said no. He was merely hoping to add to the excitement of the evening, and had no intentions of hurting Fidel Castro or anybody else. Merlino and Weber busted him for possession of a dangerous weapon. Bomb Squad cops disagreed with Feller's assessment of his home-brewed explosive. There was a concrete wall between Castro and where Feller had planned to detonate his bomb, and the barrier would have kept the Cuban from getting hurt. But for the cops assigned to protect him and the crowd in attendance, it would have been a different story.[52]

As Castro's speech was winding down, and with the rally about to break up, Weber and Merlino hustled Feller into a van and out of the park. The public didn't learn of the threat until the next day, and it made a difference; with tensions already sky-high a possible panic had been avoided. Informed by cops of the incident when he finally stopped talking, Castro shrugged it off without comment. He was supposed to show up later at a ball sponsored by one of the Spanish-language newspapers, but cops convinced him to scrub the appearance.

A subsequent search of Feller's room turned up a bag full of the sulphur-zinc mix and more pieces of aluminum tubing. He told police that about a year previous, he had detonated one of his big firecrackers at the carousel in the park, and it hadn't done much. Improving his technique with practice, he fashioned another one and enjoyed a much bigger bang.[53]

Feller turned out to be a bored nut job with some odd ideas about fun, and he wasn't a member of any anti-Castro group. But his idiotic misadventure provided a genuine threat where before only a phony one had existed; the Massachusetts native was a clueless dupe of the Castro propaganda machine. Thus a pattern was established: The fabricated threats would multiply and intensify over the next years, until it seemed the United States had no choice but to help Fidel complete this self-fulfilling prophecy. And the name of Frank Weber, an ordinary Manhattan detective, was going to figure large in future American-Cuban relations.

3

THE TAMALES
STEP UP

The FBI received some assistance from an unlikely source in the spring of 1959. Meyer Lansky, in some respects not much at odds with the intellectual tradition of his neighbors on Manhattan's Upper West Side (at least he liked to see himself that way), was a daily reader of the *New York Times*. Referring to Herbert Matthews's reporting, Robert Lacey, Lansky's biographer, said that it was "doing much to influence American opinion. But the friendly and reasonable regime about which Meyer was reading did not correspond to the Fidel Castro whose officials were locking up [Lansky's] brother without a trial. He came to feel that American opinion was dangerously out of touch with the way things were really moving in Cuba."[1] On May 22, 1959, Lansky met with FBI officials in Fort Lauderdale, with an eye toward setting the record straight.

Lansky admitted from the start that there was a self-serving aspect to his analysis, i.e., that the Communists were bad for business. And they were. Still, he thought the United States government should be brought up to speed on the evolving situation before Cuba became a real threat. Lansky lived outside of and beyond the reach of the law for most of his life. But as evidenced by his wartime intelligence contributions, he considered himself a patriot. And Lansky, who spoke to agents including Dennis O'Shea for almost an hour, advanced his theory that because Castro had Communists in such high-ranking posts, the entire government would soon be in Communist hands. The meeting came to a close with the casino owner offering his services toward gathering more information. Meyer Lansky, mob boss, professional gambler, political scientist, and would-be FBI informant got the cold shoulder from the bureau.[2]

Not far away, in Cuba, and at around this same time, Santo Trafficante was having a different set of problems. He was tossed into a detention center at Trescornia, where he was held for some time with other mobbed-down casino men like Meyer Lansky's brother, Jake. It wasn't so bad. They let him out to attend his daughter's wedding, and, "They would let anybody come in. They would let anybody stay with us until 12 o'clock at night. We would cook, we would have food brought in, we would drink and . . . sometimes, the guards would come and sit down with us and eat. Some meals it was like one big happy family. I really had a rest there, if you want to know the truth. I enjoyed it. It was cool, too, in the evening."[3]

Though this son of the Tampa and Havana rackets didn't beef about his incarceration, he had seen the handwriting on the wall, and it was in big block letters. After recouping the back pay of those restless casino employees, Castro ordered the gambling operations shuttered for good, and Santo, among others, looked for a permanent exit.

Meyer Lansky and Santo Trafficante were not the only big names disabused of whatever neutral ideas they might have held regarding the Castro movement. Close to the same period that Lansky met with FBI agents in Fort Lauderdale, Errol Flynn returned to Cuba to limn the stinker *Cuban Rebel Girls,* a cinematic sop to Castro and his revolution. Flynn had become a great favorite of Fidel's with his sympathetic newspaper stories during the revolution. "But in early May," Flynn's biographer Jeffrey Myers wrote in *Inherited Risk,* "after he'd returned to make his pro-Castro movie, the FBI reported that he'd been harshly interrogated by the Cuban secret police." The romantic notions that the actor once held were knocked out of him by Castro's thugs, who reminded him of the Gestapo: he was taken aback by their hatred of Americans. He was appalled, too, by the new regime's casual practice of capital punishment and the hit men Castro hired to kill his enemies. "I was all enthused and under the impression that this was a revolution, to quote Castro, 'the purest and gentlest in the world.' There is one thing to start a revolution, another to win it, and still another to make it stick, and as far as this writer is concerned it ain't sticking," Flynn said. "The police state of Cuba is not very different from that of its predecessors."[4]

In late 1959, rumors swirled through the swelling Cuban exile community of an organized strike against the Castro government. The rumblings had quiet beginnings, but as the weeks went by, they got louder. By the first months of 1960, the alleged action had burgeoned into plans for a full-scale takeover of the island. Invasion plans could have originated with those Batistianos who had landed in the United States when the dictator's government crashed. Chief among them was a character named Rolando Masferrer, who fled to Miami aboard his yacht, holding seventeen million dollars in cash (it was confiscated instantly).[5] His nefarious activities were so numerous and so richly textured that no story set against this background can ignore him. Masferrer was an official in Batista's government, a senator and a virulent anti-Communist with strong ties to the military. He was believed to be responsible for the torture and imprisonment of hundreds of

Cubans who opposed Batista. FBI intelligence from this period stated that Masferrer was the proud owner of a decommissioned U.S. Navy PT boat that he had purchased for his personal use a few years earlier. It was this PT boat that Masferrer was said, or was said to have said, to be employing for a series of strikes against Castro.[6]

These first whispers had Masferrer and his confederates purchasing arms throughout the United States for shipment to Florida. But the most persistent story had the former Cuban senator deploying frogmen with underwater demolition experience to attack tunnels, bridges, and the like in and around Havana. This alleged sabotage was supposed to have been executed in mid-1959, but it never happened.[7]

The Tamale Squad, with assists from the Jacksonville and New York field offices, was obligated to run down these leads. The contacts they debriefed were usually described as people who had "furnished reliable information in the past." The hope was that such sources could either confirm or dispel the talk that grew more insistent each day, thrilling anti-Castroites with predictions of a quick downfall for Fidel.

Exile hopes were buoyed by a dirtier story. Commenting on intelligence picked up through a New York source, FBI Director J. Edgar Hoover warned of a coming "Cuban counterrevolutionary movement led by [name redacted, but identified in other documents as Rolando Masferrer] prominent anti-Castro leader in Miami, Florida, who has approximately 3,000 men in training throughout Florida. Agents have been purchasing weapons in the United States which are to be transported to undisclosed training camps in Florida."[8]

The Florida group was not acting alone. Other forces were massing in Mexico and the Dominican Republic, the supposed source of the money, and this "three-prong invasion force will simultaneously attack Cuba at three undisclosed locations." The Dominican-based group was report-edly the biggest and the best trained, but their numbers were creating a headache for Trujillo, who "requested the with-drawal of the United States naval mission so that invasion preparations would not be observed. Preliminary invasion plans include destruction of Cuban sugar refineries by air at-tacks, and if this fails, consideration would then be given to destruction of these plantations by sabotage." The launch date was scheduled for between January 15 and January 30 and "inquiries," the director signed off, "are being conducted concerning this matter and you will be furnished any addi-tional pertinent information developed."[9]

It would have been impossible to keep the screws down on a story as explosive as this one, and the lid blew off on De-cember 29, 1959, with an article in the *New York Times*. Citing *Revolución*, the house organ of the Castro government, and under a headline stating "Invasion of Cuba Called Immi-nent," the *Times* reported that Castro believed, or would have liked to have others believe, that the attack was coming from Mexico, the Dominican Republic, and Miami. *Revolución* threw in Nicaragua, Haiti, Honduras, and Guatemala as ad-ditional staging areas.

But Castro's intelligence people had the same problem as the FBI. Everybody heard the same rumors. The details pub-lished in the *Times* piece, again with attribution to *Revolucion*, show a remarkable overlap with ongoing and contemporary FBI summaries,[10] including reports that German mercenaries were involved.[11] Castro, of course, could not stop there. The Cubans also accused the despised United Fruit Company of complicity in the plot, "protecting the plotters, helping them to get planes, boats and arms for the attack." United Fruit hotly denied the allegations and, for his part, so did the Hon-duran president.[12]

An undated bureau "airtel" dutifully recited everything the reader had picked up from the *Times* and responsibly attributed the sourcing to *Revolución*. No comment on the veracity of any of the charges though, just a cryptic note advising that additional copies of said document were being submitted for legal attachés, or "legats" in bureau-ese, stationed in Havana and Mexico.[13]

Back and forth it went, into the winter of 1960; Jacksonville (a hotbed of former Batista henchmen) to Miami, Miami to New York, New York to Washington. South Florida informants sounded incredulous notes when squeezed by the Tamales to bring some certainty to the chatter. A Miami source suggested that there might have been maybe 200 men in the Dominican Republic and about the same number in Mexico, but certainly no more than 300 in either place, and in any event, they weren't all responsible to Masferrer. The same source noted that there were definitely not 3,000 men in Florida or anywhere else in training.[14]

Under an addendum headlined ACTION, FBI Assistant Director F. J. Baumgardner opined that "This may prove to be one of the numerous rumors which have been circulated recently regarding invasion plans to take place around 1–1–60." He concluded, a bit wearily perhaps, "We are pursuing the investigation to determine if there is such a plan, and identify the individuals who may be connected with any such endeavor."[15]

Unfortunately for the SAC of the New York Office, J. Edgar Hoover did not truck in white-hot rumors that could not be substantiated. In a communication dated January 18, 1960, headlined and underscored PERSONAL ATTENTION, the director referred to those 3,000 men allegedly training in Florida. "You were instructed," he wrote, "to initiate immediate investigation to determine if there was any basis for the allegation and if so whether a violation of neutrality statutes under our jurisdiction existed. You were instructed that this matter must be vigorously pursued, resolved promptly and a report submitted to the Bureau [meaning *me*—J. Edgar was the 'bureau' the way the 'court' is the judge] by January 11, 1960." Evidently, this hadn't happened.

New York got a good old-fashioned ass-chewing. Hoover stated that "A review submitted pursuant to this request demonstrates the lack of any positive and forthright investigation to resolve this matter." The Director mocked a previously generated report that included as "intelligence" the *New York Times* piece of December 29. "It appears that the information contained in this report is of little value so far as developing evidence that the original allegation is true or unfounded.

"The Department [of State] and interested agencies have been furnished the original allegations which if true are of extreme concern to this Government and therefore, must be promptly resolved. The Bureau will not tolerate routine handling or lackadaisical approach to the investigation in this case which could conceivably *embarrass the Bureau.**

"You are instructed, therefore, to initiate immediate positive investigation in this matter and advise the Bureau no later than January 22, 1960, on the step you are taking and the investigation contemplated to bring this case to a logical conclusion as promptly as possible."[16]

Meanwhile, the Castro government was intent on hurrying Batista officials to face its firing squads. Those who

---

*The emphasis is the author's. "Embarrassing the bureau" was the most cardinal of sins that anyone associated with the FBI could commit. It was unspoken law among agents, and Hoover's use of this phrase would have made it understood precisely how serious he was.

managed to escape Cuba, Fidel wanted back. He was especially hot on getting higher-ranking military officers repatriated so that he could put them on trial (or not) and have
them executed. Rolando Masferrer fit into that category.
Separate from any invasion rumors that Fidel might have
heard, as far as he was concerned, Masferrer was guilty of
war crimes. The Revolution wanted to get its hands on him.

By the spring of 1960 the Tamale Squad, with Special
Agent Bill Holloman in the foreground, was closing the gap
on their intelligence deficit with the help of sources cultivated on both sides of the fight. Holloman developed a lead
that two agents from the Cuban intelligence organization,
G2, had slipped into the States with a mission: kidnap Masferrer, get him back to Cuba and into Castro's custody.

Holloman went undercover as a corrupt Dade County
sheriff's deputy and made contact with G2. He told them he
wanted to help, and a meeting was set for a motel near the
airport. The room was wired so that other Tamale Squad reg-
ulars could hear what was going on, and Holloman baited
the Cubans into specific language that would show their un-
equivocal conspiracy to kidnap. Once that was accomplished, Holloman was to deliver a signal word and the
arrest would be made.

The Cubans committed. Holloman gave the signal. But he
was supposed to leave the door unlocked. He hadn't. As ca-
sually as he could under the pressure, Holloman sidled over
and unlatched the door. The Tamale Squad burst into the
room, fell on the hapless Cubans, and apprehended them.
They were subsequently deported.[17]

The bureau's investigation of this Masferrer-led invasion
had intensified through the winter of 1960. With the
planned date for the attack having come and gone, agents in

New York, Miami, Jacksonville, and in the Washington, D.C., field office fanned out, squeezing law enforcement sources and Cuban exiles for a definitive word on the go-date and details.

There was no shortage of anti-Castro groups that warranted investigation, but they were fragmented in a way that reflected the politics of their homeland. For every recent refugee from Cuba, there seemed to be a corresponding exile group. One organization, called the Cubana Institucionalista de Portuondo, or CIP, was strongly anti-Castro but limited its activities to propaganda and politics. One source familiar with the group told agents that they were, in fact, preparing for the "liberation" of Cuba and their eventual return to that country, but the source said that would most likely be accomplished through American intervention, and that in any event, the group did not traffic in arms; they were not men of war.[18]

In a report dated February 1, 1960, the Jacksonville field office filed a summary of an exhaustive investigation conducted out of its headquarters. The SAC came to this conclusion: A failure to "indicate that there is any activity in connection with the training of troops or collecting of arms in connection with" an alleged invasion of Cuba.[19] An unnamed Tamale Squad member weighed in with an extensive recap of his crew's efforts and wrote that various informants could provide no definitive answers regarding any invasion. "[One] informant stated that he knew of no such force of 3,000 anywhere in Florida or anywhere else, and doubted that an army of that size could be assembled even by combining all the anti-Castro groups currently in the area."[20] Another source opined that there had been talk of such plans since about 12:01 A.M. on January 1, 1959, and still another said that nothing was going to happen until all the anti-Castro factions achieved some kind of unification. And as far as having 3,000 soldiers together, this man stated that Masferrer would be lucky to put together 300. Masferrer, "like many others in the anti-Castro groups, was given to a large amount of talk, but very little action."[21] Considering that this thing was supposed to come off during the last weeks of January 1960, and in light of the fact that it was now February, the source continued, then most, if not all, of the arms and the soldiers would have to be in place. It would have been virtually impossible to keep an action this big and this exciting a secret.

The Tamales were keeping tabs on another shadowy group, *Milicias Anticommunistas Obreras y Campesinas* (Laborers and Farmers Anti-Communist Militia), or the MAOC. Back in January, Miami had developed information that the MAOC needed a thousand men, "and that the problems of automatic weapons, arms and supplies, and the evacuation of the wounded from Cuba had been solved. There was no specific date mentioned for any invasion." The MAOC was formed for one reason—"to fight in Cuba"—but again, it looks like this group was better at talking than it was at mobilizing for war. "The primary purpose," a source said of all MAOC meetings, "is the indoctrination of the members in methods in which communism may be combated and how it can be recognized."[22] In other words, another political organization long on assembling and speechifying.

Coupled with the dogged efforts of the New York office, the Tamale Squad developed extensive information on who Rolando Masferrer was and what he was alleged to have been doing into the winter of 1960. Masferrer owned a boat, it was true, a boat that he and others had used to flee Cuba upon Batista's fall. The vessel, which Masferrer was then desperately trying to sell without success, was safely at anchor in the Miami River. And rather than lead any army in an invasion, Masferrer was busy scrambling around Miami trying to borrow money to buy groceries.[23] F. J. Baumgardner, the beleaguered F.B.I. assistant director, signed off on a report dated April 22, 1960, with this definitive statement: "In view of the fact that previous investigation has failed to substantiate any of the original allegations in this matter and since all logical leads have been covered, this case will be placed in a closed status, UACB [unless advised to the contrary by the bureau]."[24]

A recurrent chord was being struck. There wasn't much that was beyond the imaginings of the Cuban exiles, but real action seemed to be beyond their grasp. With a boundless romanticism borne of despair, they could talk and drink and plan and dream, without much connection to reality. In their defense, it's impossible to ascertain whether any of these "plans" were ever real. Later speculation centered on Castro himself as the source of the rumors, a smoke screen intended to whip up anti-Cuban sentiment within the United States. Fidel could then identify his enemies. He seemed to take the opposite lesson from the boy who cried wolf: the real threat to the safety and the happiness of the Cuban people was coming from the United States, not from his revolution.

4

DIPLOMATIC IMMUNITY OR PERSONA NON GRATA

Dwight David Eisenhower defeated the Democratic Party's presidential candidate, Adlai Stevenson, twice; the first time in 1952, then for good measure again in 1956. The 1960 presidential campaign was getting cranked up. There would be no incumbent in this race, and by 1959, Richard Nixon, Ike's vice president, seemed to have the inside track on the Republican nomination. Nixon wasn't a lock, but his only serious competition was being mounted by New York governor Nelson Rockefeller.

The contest for the Democratic nomination was tighter. Some thought that Stevenson wanted to be nudged into another race. Other contenders were Stuart Symington, the Missouri senator, Lyndon B. Johnson, the senate majority leader from Texas, and Hubert H. Humphrey, the Minnesota senator. The junior senator from Massachusetts, John Fitzgerald Kennedy, also emerged to jockey for consideration. Besides youth, inexperience, and the widespread opinion that his rich daddy was going to buy him the nomination, Kennedy had two hurdles to clear: his Catholicism and, as the party pendulum took a progressive swing in the congressional elections of 1958, his peculiar lack of liberal credentials.[1] None of this was about to stand in the way of JFK. He had ambition to burn.

Kennedy was wise to the press right from the first. Announcing on Saturday, January 2, 1960, when little else was happening in D.C., he was sure to get maximum media exposure. He sounded a couple of vague platitudes, and he mentioned ending the arms race. But he made it clear that a Kennedy administration would focus on the fight for democratic principles in the third world.[2]

It had been fourteen short months since Fidel Castro swept away the rotting regime of Fulgencio Batista, eleven since he had taken a victory lap around New York and Washington, and it was a scant eight weeks after John F. Kennedy announced his presidential aspirations. Diplomatic relations between Cuba and the United States were about to take a nosedive. The freighter *Le Coubre,* originating from Belgium, sailing under a French tricolor, and loaded with weapons for the Cuban revolution, exploded in Havana Harbor. Seventy-five Cubans were killed and another two hundred were injured. An eerie reminiscence of the burning of the *Maine* fifty years earlier was impossible to avoid.[3]

Castro wasted no time in labeling the incident an act of sabotage. He blamed the United States. There was no evidence of dirty business on the part of the Americans or anybody else, and none was developed.[4] Almost everybody agreed that it was an accident. But in an incendiary speech, Castro said of the United States, "You will reduce us neither by war nor famine," and the government-controlled press went on the offensive against the United States.[5] Historians seem to agree that U.S.-Cuban relations passed the "point of no return" after the incident.[6] It isn't clear whether Eisenhower officials and Ike himself had been hoping that Fidel would merely go away, but they threatened to take drastic economic action against Castro's government by ending the sugar quota, the amount of cane product it bought from Cuba every year. By mid-March, the Americans were still mulling the ramifications of their threat.[7]

Yet the rampant allegations of red influence on the Castro government and differing opinions on whether or not Castro himself was a Communist were becoming increasingly beside the point. The political season was about to get underway in the United States, and Cuba loomed as a hot-button issue. Ike had a problem. Liberals within the foreign service had long lamented Batista's abuses for many reasons, including the theory that his brutality was sowing the seeds of a left-wing backlash. As early as 1958, one Eisenhower official was quoted as saying, "If Batista was bad medicine for everybody, Castro would be worse."[8] By the time *Le Coubre* blew up, their worst fears, stoked by their own inaction, were coming true.

The U.S. Department of State, in a gesture seen widely as an olive branch to the Castro government, had some months before appointed Philip Bonsal as ambassador to Cuba. Bonsal was supposed to represent the liberal point of view, and to demonstrate to Castro that the United States wanted to work with the Cuban government toward the goal of normalized relations. But American diplomatic machinations proved fruitless. The line appeared to have been drawn, and Castro was not of a mind to alter it.[9]

Serious observers have settled on an explanation for Castro's indifference and his tough talk. If Eisenhower officials misread the signals, it stemmed from their view of the world and the role of their country in that world. Castro wasn't about to knuckle under to U.S. pressure or swoon for American sweet talk. The hurdle was ego. There was no way Fidel could define himself as a thorn in the American lion's paw, attain the global admiration he thought was his due, and still be buddies with the United States of America.[10]

Anecdotal accounts of Castro's abuses piled up, and by mid-1960, disillusionment in Cuba had taken hold. There were a hundred thousand people on a waiting list just to *apply* for visas to go to the United States.[11]

"We had such high hopes," a friend told American diplomat Wayne Smith at dinner shortly after Castro had assumed power. "We thought that at last Cuba might have its first honest and democratic government, and one, moreover, which put the welfare of the people first. Now we see it is not to be. We have traded one dictatorship for another."[12]

Castro had support, no question, but there was just as much virulent opposition. Cubans against his "reforms" included working men and women, even those who had been previous supporters. The edges were starting to fray. But Castro clung to some popularity, if only because Cubans so desperately wanted his revolution to succeed. "Such sharp differences of opinion were bound to produce personal conflicts throughout the society. Families were divided," according to Smith. "Classmates fought on school grounds. Frequent fights, sometimes near riots, erupted in bars and other public places."[13]

The Eisenhower administration sought avenues of action. By March of 1960, the CIA had drawn up a paper titled "A Program of Covert Action Against the Castro Regime." This was the four-point plan:

A. Formation of a Cuban exile organization to attract Cuban loyalties, to direct opposition activities, and to provide cover for Agency operations
B. A propaganda offensive in the name of the opposition
C. Creation inside Cuba of a clandestine intelligence collection and action apparatus to be responsive to the direction of the exile organization
D. Development outside Cuba of a small paramilitary force to be introduced into Cuba to organize, train, and lead resistance groups.[14]

On March 17, Eisenhower approved the plan. The Cuba Project, as it came to be known, was a sanctioned go. Though he admits he was far too junior to have had any influence at all on the decisions being made, Wayne Smith and other diplomats had grave misgivings about the project's success.

CIA operative E. Howard Hunt (the "E" stands for Everette) was in on the plan from the jump. An attorney's son, Hunt came of age in the upstate New York town of Hamburg. He graduated from Brown University and during the early part of World War II served aboard a destroyer in the North Atlantic. An injury prohibited him from further naval action, but while recuperating stateside, Hunt felt sure that he could still make a contribution to the country's war effort. Right around this time, General William "Wild Bill" Donovan was organizing an independent covert military organization that would become known as the Office of Strategic Services, or OSS. Through some contacts his father had, Hunt went through the appropriate channels and before long found himself in the Far East with the OSS. Later, he worked as a correspondent for *Life* magazine, and as a filmmaker he documented the Marshall Plan reconstruction of Vienna.[15]

Reconstituted from the remnants of Donovan's OSS and brought to life under Harry Truman in 1947, the Central Intelligence Agency was by this time headed up by OSS veteran Allen Dulles, a Wall Street lawyer and pipe-puffing patrician who was also John Foster Dulles's brother. Howard Hunt was a charter member of this new intelligence organization. By the time the Cuba thing rolled around, Hunt was quite naturally excited to be called in on it, though one of Smith's colleagues at State, evidently expressing department-wide reservations, cautioned him, "I hope you're not going to get into any of this Cuba business."[16]

It was now May of 1960. Francis Gary Powers, piloting the ultrasecret U-2 spy plane, had been shot down over the Soviet Union. To the amazement of all and the consternation of Hunt, Powers had parachuted safely to earth. Hunt had hoped that with regard to their Cuban work, kindred spirits at CIA would bring their influence to bear on "liberal elements of the government." But CIA was scrambling to cover its ass in the wake of this diplomatic debacle. The Cuba Project was temporarily slowed.[17]

Under a flimsy cover, Hunt embarked on a walking tour of Havana. "The atmosphere of repression struck me almost at once," he wrote in *Give Us This Day*, his memoir of the period. "Uniformed *barbudos* with carelessly slung Czech burp guns guarded hotels and other confiscated property. I walked to the Malecon and saw long lines of Cubans waiting outside our consulate for visas to the U.S. From there I turned back to Sloppy Joe's where I lunched on draft beer and a poor boy sandwich, alone at the great bar where once you had to fight for service. Now only ghosts and memories filled the big room; the place was desolate, the bartenders sullen. The uncertainties of Batista days had given way to the nightmare of Castroism."[18]

E. Howard Hunt with his cold, gimlet eye was not gulled by press reports or made giddy with romanticism over conquering heroes of the left. He had no illusions to be disabused of. So thoroughly disheartened by what he found in Havana, Hunt was seized with the mounting feeling that CIA was on the right course in Cuba. Recalling another evening afoot in the Cuban capital, he wrote, "I strolled through a downtown park and stopped to listen to José Pardo Llada harangue the crowd. In true revolutionary style, this vicious radio propagandist and apologist for Castro, set the crowd on half a dozen of the better dressed element who fled screaming down the street pursued by half a hundred *Castristas*. What happened to them I never knew. Men and women disappeared without notice, their bodies ended in limed common graves. This, I told myself, was the fresh wind of change that was purging the corruption and oppression from the Pearl of the Antilles.

"If I had doubts about the wisdom of our Cuban Project, they were resolved that night and I determined to dedicate myself to ridding Cuba of Castro and his henchmen, regardless of personal cost and effort."[19]

The growing Miami population now numbered about 250,000, about 40,000 of whom were Cuban exiles, and more were arriving every day, by fishing boat, hijacked airliner, and stolen crop duster.[20]

The increasingly shrill tone between Washington and Havana was creating a static that was playing itself out on the streets of Miami. With Moscow and Havana exchanging diplomatic visits, and the announcement that Soviet Premier Nikita Khrushchev had accepted the invitation of the Castro government and was slated to visit Cuba, tensions between pro- and anti-Castro elements were ratcheted up another notch.

One June afternoon, Miami cops were dispatched to the corner of NE First St. and Flagler Ave, near the building where the Cuban consulate was housed. A protest was being staged by a group calling itself the Anti-Communist Liberation Front. Two hundred demonstrators took turns winding each other up with chants and slogans. Somebody drove up with a trunkful of placards lettered with pithy slogans like "Castro, Human Butcher of Cuba," and "Fidel, The Killer of Democracy." Nervous cops called for reinforcements. The order to disperse the crowd was radioed over from headquarters, and police succeeded, briefly, before the demonstrators regrouped across the street from the consulate. Fourteen men were arrested, and the paddy wagon pulled away to the lilting strains of "El Combate," a patriotic hymn. Everybody got lucky that day. Real violence was avoided.[21] But as the summer wound down, one weary cop said, "I don't care how you slice it, the exiles are ready to fight, even on our streets."[22]

One hotspot was Paula's Restaurant, a block away from the Federal Building downtown. The place was owned by Jose Manuel Paula, fifty-eight years old in 1960 and a former boxing promoter, and his wife, Maria. Both were staunch Castroites. Back in the day when Fidel himself was a Miami exile, Paula's was his hangout. Paula's was a natural magnet for Fidelistas, with one Castro publication dubbing the place "an unconquerable trench of the revolution."[23]

Bill Kelly remembered the restaurant well: "This one day, some guy comes by in the morning with a concrete block and throws it through the plate glass window. Joe's a little upset. He gets a glazier, who comes and puts a new window in. About lunchtime, somebody, maybe the same guy, comes back with another concrete block, knocks out the second window. So he gets the glazier to come back and put in a third window, all in one day, with a steel mesh screen in front of it, which would not allow a concrete block to come through." Paula's had by that time acquired the well-deserved reputation as a flash point between pro- and anti-Castro elements, and it was the setting for many a brawl. The proprietor's preventive measures and resourcefulness enraged the Fidelhaters even more.

"Seven or eight o'clock at night, there's a crowd in the restaurant having dinner," Kelly said. "Two anti-Castro people come in the front door. One of them is carrying a Thompson submachine gun with about a twenty-round clip in it. The other guy's got a .45 caliber Colt.

"On the far wall, hanging high up is a [portrait] of Fidel Castro, even before he had a beard. Big thing, much bigger than life-size. These two guys open up on this [picture] with the machine gun and the pistol," as patrons presumably scrambled for cover. "Guess what?" Kelly said, "They not only didn't hit Fidel, they didn't even hit the frame." It was a miracle no one was hurt, but Paula's partisans pegged this as a different kind of divine intervention: Fidel Castro was protected from all evil.[24]

Mrs. Paula felt the couple needed to take more active measures, and, maybe based on the disgraceful marksmanship of her enemies, she and her husband decided to take up target shooting.[25]

The *Miami Herald*, whose editorial pages had been maintaining a wariness toward Castro, came down hard on the regime on June 7, 1960. "The Castro government," the writer opined, "has gone too far—with its open wooing of Soviet Russia, Red China, and all the enemies of the free world—to back down now.

Dr. Castro is learning the lesson that must be learned bitterly by every dictator—that the path of dictatorship, of malice and lies, of distortions and repressions, must be traveled downhill, with no brakes."

The piece went on to describe Ambassador Bonsal's mission as "futile," and warned that "in these worrisome and dangerous times the Cuban gadfly at the heart of the hemisphere assumes a nuisance value beyond its puny might. There is the growing feeling that the safety of the hemisphere calls for a challenge to Cuba's headlong course," and suggested that the Organization of American States would be the appropriate place for that to occur.[26]

A s Hunt's opinion calcified and the first fitful shakings of the Cuba Project gained momentum, diplomacy between the United States and Cuba entered a deep freeze. On the evening of June 15, 1960, after meeting with a group of Cubans, two American embassy employees were collared by Cuban military intelligence agents on a Havana street.[27] Edwin L. Sweet and William G. Friedemann were accused of conspiring with "counterrevolutionists" and "gravely affecting the national sovereignty of Cuba by interfering in its internal affairs."[28]

Officially, Sweet and Friedemann were "legal attachés." Unofficially, they were agents of the Federal Bureau of Investigation.

Ed Sweet was driving his car through the Havana rain. He was idling at a traffic light when somebody walked up on the driver's side of his car and stuck a pistol in his face. The guy told him to get out.

Sweet said, "Who're you?"

"Get out of the car," the man repeated. He tried the door handle.

Sweet hit the gas and shook the guy loose, but the Cuban fired a pot shot at him as Sweet was pursued by several other vehicles that forced him to the curb. The drivers got out and drew their weapons, and Sweet spotted Friedemann being walked across the street, also in the custody of Castro agents.

"I produced my diplomatic carnet from the Cuban Foreign Office and declared I was a diplomat and that they had no right to detain me if they were officers, which fact I doubted in view of their conduct. A fat, red-faced individual shoved his cocked .45 automatic against my head."[29]

Howard Hunt watched the whole thing go down. He was just coming back from a restaurant when he spotted Sweet in his car, and was about to go over and say hello when Castro's men swooped down on Sweet and hauled him away. Figuring he was next, Hunt turned his face to the wall and slipped back into the gathering crowd.[30]

The Cubans forced the FBI men into a car and drove them to the headquarters of the Department of Investigations of the Rebel Army, known by the Spanish acronym DIER, and known by Sweet to be Communist controlled. Sweet demanded to speak to the American embassy and was told that DIER agents would make the call themselves, when they were ready.

"A red-bearded man [with the nom de guerre of Major Fury], a Communist married to an American woman, and whose complete name is known to our office, advised us that once in the DIER headquarters, there is no such thing as diplomats."

Good thing, too, because the treatment the DIER thugs dished out to Sweet and Friedemann was a far shot from diplomatic. The fat man who arrested them had that .45 shoved into a pants pocket and stuck it under Sweet's nose when the spirit moved him, and the spirit moved him frequently.

Sweet refused to submit to a personal search and said that if his abductors wanted to see what he had on him, the five of them should be enough to do the job, and when they tried to take his picture, he let them know that wasn't going to happen either.

"You refuse to be photographed by the police laboratory?"

Sweet told them, "It would take more Cubans than they could get into that small space to get me in front of the camera.

"They then removed me to an interview room. At this point an individual sat down directly across the room and began playing with a Czech machine gun. He lined the gun up in what appeared to be about the center of my chest and methodically racked the bolt back putting a cartridge into the barrel. Then he removed the clip, threw out the cartridge, let the bolt fly forward and pulled the trigger . . . 25 or 30 times."

DIER didn't have much luck getting a snapshot of Ed Sweet. He kept his head down and his hand in front of his face, seated on a couch, and the photographer, dressed in a rebel army uniform, flopped on the floor and attempted to point his camera up. Enter Raúl Castro, the "effeminate appearing" brother of Fidel. Raul remarked sarcastically that he hoped the Americans were enjoying the courteous treatment they had been receiving, and that they appreciated the fact that their diplomatic immunity was being respected. Raúl next took the opportunity to launch into a boilerplate party line harangue "regarding monopolies, power, North American interests, Wall Street, and a bunch of jibber jabber regarding poor, humble Cuba. He stated Cuba was unable to afford spies like the FBI and CIA but, nevertheless, the revolutionary government has the support of the people and we were meddling in Cuba's internal affairs, engaged in conspiracy against Cuba and committing acts of espionage."

Raúl said he knew all about Ed Sweet. The American had a long history as a spy in Mexico and Guatemala and was known not just to the government, but to the Cuban people, too. (Sweet later commented that Raúl had been more or less on the money.)

The Cuban didn't slow down for any edgewise words. "I will not have you shot," he said, "but will expel you from the country immediately. When you come back with the Marines I will kill you then."

After Raúl's tirade was exhausted, Sweet and Friedemann were loaded into a car and escorted by motorcade to the American embassy. They went straight to work on a lengthy message to the FBI and hand-delivered it to the Western Union office at Obispo Street, standing over the telegrapher's shoulder long enough to ascertain that the cable was indeed being sent.

Sweet noticed a blue and gray Buick he was sure he'd seen before following them as the agents left the location. They circled several Havana blocks, and as the sun came up on the sixteenth of June, doubled back to the Western Union office. The clerk was still working on their message.[31] Declared persona non grata, Special Agents Edwin Sweet and William Friedemann were given twenty-four hours to get out of Cuba.[32]

By 8:05 A.M. the Cuban radio station *Rebelde*, a Castro organ, was reporting that two Americans who were conspiring with antigovernment elements had been arrested the night before, and in later dispatches, they were named and identified as employees of the American embassy.[33]

The American embassy telegrammed Washington at noon the next day and informed the State Department that American diplomats in Havana were making a "vigorous written protest" to the Ministry of Foreign Relations. They also issued a press release and the predictable uproar ensued.[34]

"A Day for Insults:" the *Miami News* declared, "Cuba Expels Two Yanks." The Havana paper *Revolución* blared, "Two American Diplomats Expelled For Conspiracy"[35] under a two-inch headline with whatever photographs DIER agents were able to muster of Sweet and Friedemann.[36] The story reported that the men had been "surprised" while plotting with counterrevolutionaries and violating Cuban sovereignty.[37]

In a memo fired off to J. Edgar Hoover, Miami SAC Lee Teague suggested he knew what kind of trouble the bureau was in with Havana, all but admitting the titles that Sweet and Friedemann carried were diplomatic cover and that they'd been blown. The memo states that the SAC would make "no further calls to Havana since it would appear we must be most circumspect in making any calls to the Legat [American Embassy]." The writer also provided the bureau with the details on "two individuals in Miami who might be declared persona non grata by the United States" and booted back to Cuba in a classic quid pro quo.[38]

The State Department was left scrambling for details. After Ambassador Bonsal filed his protest with the Cuban Foreign Ministry, he contacted the FBI, knowing that the bureau by this time had a complete background report. A turf skirmish followed. Their interests just weren't the same.

Alan Belmont had a reputation among his fellow FBI agents as a man of impeccable integrity, and, according to former agents, was relied upon for his sure-handedness. In a memo dated June 16, Belmont wrote to fellow assistant director Parsons about Bonsal, who was pressing the bureau for details on the action against his agents, that, "State Department will just have to wait until we get the facts on this." The FBI knew the Cubans were "laying for our Legat personnel." And Belmont finished his memo by saying, "We do not intend to furnish State Department full background on our activities in Cuba."[39]

Bonsal was most likely—and understandably—trying to save face, but Belmont, still bristling, got himself cranked up again later that same day. "I think we should go on an immediate and strong counter-offensive," he wrote. "This can be done by having State Department issue a release to the effect that this action in Cuba is apparently retaliation for action the U.S. government has found it necessary to take against the criminal activities of Castro agents in the U.S.—for example, the attempt on the part of Cuban agents to kidnap Rolando Masferrer in Miami, for which two Cuban agents are currently under indictment and awaiting trial." He wholeheartedly approved Lee Teague's suggestion in Miami that the United States expel a pair of Cubans in fair exchange, and went on to furnish his boss with the names.[40]

The next day, in what could have been a reference that dated back to George Davis's opinion on Fidel Castro from 1956, Belmont added, "We have previously warned the State Department [about] the Cuban government," and that while American diplomats were wringing their hands over the wording in a reinforcement of its protest to Cuban authorities, they were now on their own. "The decision as to what the note shall contain," Belmont wrote with some smugness, "is the responsibility of the State Department."[41]

Back on American soil, Ed Sweet filed a follow-up report to FBI headquarters. Dated June 20 and addressed to Belmont, Sweet offered these observations on the shifting political scene in Cuba: "Cuban employees in the Embassy congratulated me and stated that being arrested by the Castro regime was a compliment rather than a shame. Several Cubans outside the sphere of Embassy influence came by my house on the night of 6–16–60 to congratulate me, to express their regret over the action taken by the ruffians acting under the Castro brothers, and to express their hope that we would indeed soon be back and an end would be brought to the present Communist domination of Cuba."

At the airport on his way out of Havana to Key West, two women working the ticket counter of Aero Vias Q, at considerable risk, shook hands with Sweet and wished him good luck. Sweet took it as an accurate barometer of his own estimation of the growing discontent on the island. "When Fidel

Castro entered into power on 1–1–59, he was believed to have 98% of the popular support in Cuba. It is now considered doubtful that he has 40% of the support."

Sweet pointed out that when Castro took over, not a single journalist opposed him, but that as of his writing, not one free newspaper existed in the country, and that as far as that 40 percent went, he named redacted names long known to the FBI for their Communist association.

As far as Special Agent Edwin Sweet was concerned, his expulsion was a badge of honor, a clear indication that the bureau was doing something right. "When the Castro regime is overthrown," he said, "it will be found that his revolutionary government only added prestige to the bureau by arresting the writer and SA Friedemann and expelling us from Cuba."[42] Repatriated to Miami, Special Agents Sweet and Friedemann went straight to work in Howard Albaugh's Tamale Squad.

Sweet's statistics can be debated, but his anecdotal evidence seems borne out by the antagonistic tone Castro took toward all things American. Fidel must have been aware that his popular support was eroding. An idol a short eighteen months before, his graven image was now perceived to have feet of clay. In any event, the gauntlet had been thrown down. Diplomacy appears to have been abandoned by both Castro and U.S. officials and as far as any rapprochement went, well, there simply wasn't going to be any. With Castro's mouthpieces shouting at the tops of their lungs and American cold warriors snarling out of the sides of their mouths, it seemed a foregone conclusion that any further diplomacy was going to be a waste of time.

5

HISTORY PRECEDES ITSELF FIRST AS FARCE

The Bizarre Saga of the Doughnut Army

Although their objective turned toward counterespionage and away from crime-stopping, and although they couldn't have appreciated it, the Tamale Squad operated during the golden age of law enforcement. The Sixties had not happened. The Supreme Court's 1965 *Miranda* decision, in which the Court determined that a suspect must be advised of his rights before being questioned by police, was the phantasm of a day that was yet to be, and it's just as well: the Tamales inhabited a darkening shade of gray.[1]

Their wiretaps dismantled and their numbers strengthened, the G-men pressured hostile Cuban expatriates to either get in line or get out of the country. A favorite method of harassment was a technique the squad called "close surveillance." Much of this direct action was taken against Castro agitators after regular working hours. The Tamales antagonized Castro sympathizers and Cuban G2 agents to the extent that the exiles' Miami life amounted to a round-the-clock headache. One reliable technique was the two A.M. home visit, agents' headlights on bright, blaring into a slumbering target's bedroom window.

One hapless Castroite was responsible for delivering *Revolución* to grocery stores and other outlets. There was nothing legal the Tamale Squad could do to prevent that, but his six-hour newspaper route expanded to eighteen once agents got on to him. Of the sad-sack deliveryman, Bill Kelly said, "We'd stop in front of him and box him in so he couldn't go backward or forward. We'd get out of our cars and leave."[2] Bill Holloman recalled their efforts with some nostalgia, too. It was like this: "They know we're there, and we're gonna *be* there twenty-four hours a day, and screw you. If you wanna get a restraining order, good luck, buddy. Those [tactics] in the right time and place are very effective."

Almost none of these cases went to court. Known Castro operatives were dogged so relentlessly that after a series of heart-to-heart talks with FBI agents, they simply gave up and went back to Cuba. After a pro-Castro agitator landed on the Tamale radar screen, "We'd go and brace him and take him around and make like we were the greatest of friends," Holloman said. Being convinced the United States of America was not the place for him, the subject was taken to the airport and put on a plane for Havana, with a specially designed FBI business card stashed in his luggage. Castro officials on the Cuban end, ransacking the bags, would inevitably find the card. And a lot of questions no doubt needed to be answered.[3]

Hoover kept Miami FBI on a long leash, and he let the Tamale Squad, under the direct supervision of Howard Albaugh, do more or less what they thought was right to crimp Castro's stateside influence. They didn't have to worry about some lawyer stepping on their toes, because they knew they had Hoover's backing and, if push came to shove, their own lawyers' at the Justice Department.

But the Tamale Squad fell victim to the law of unintended consequences. Their efforts were so effective that the influence of Castro agents attempting to infiltrate U.S-based anti-Communist groups was negligible. The July 26 Movement in Miami was losing steam, particularly as an increasing number of anti-Castro elements arrived in the United States. Now the FBI had to deal with the reverse problem: the Wild West mentality of Castro haters.

By the summer of 1960, the Miami papers were running near-daily accounts of efforts by various "invasion" teams, who, bound for Cuba in something that floated (for a little while, anyway), had to be plucked from the Florida Strait by Coast Guard patrol boats. Armed with a pistol or a Molotov cocktail, sobriety and sanity somewhat in doubt before they set sail, these men were becoming an increasing source of frustration to the United States.

The Cuban air force suffered widespread defection under Castro. With many of its pilots now residing in Miami, and with access to one of hundreds of Florida airstrips, anti-Castroites would charter planes, violate Cuban airspace, and push out sandbags or wrenches or whatever else was on board as ordnance. Leaflet drops decrying the corrupt revolution and demanding a free Cuba occurred with alarming frequency. They were also illegal.[4] An immigration official appearing before a Senate appropriations subcommittee in June 1960 requested two million dollars to begin a program of securing these airfields to prevent any more misguided adventures. But in any event, one U.S. senator predicted that Castro would most likely be history in six months' time.[5]

One early military defector was Pedro Diaz Lanz. He also happened to be, at the time of his defection, the head of the Cuban air force. Pressed into Communist-indoctrination classes led by Raúl Castro, Diaz Lanz lashed out publicly at the Castro government and "against every type of dictatorship." Naturally, the commander's days in Havana were numbered, and after the ensuing dressing down by Castro and orders not to return to his position, Diaz Lanz fled to Miami.[6]

He returned a few months later for a spectacular flight over Havana. Frank Sturgis, the daring pilot and arms smuggler to Castro during the revolution, had also by this time turned against his former friend. Sturgis was sitting in the copilot's seat. Diaz Lanz opened the doors on the bomb bay of his B–25 and showered downtown Havana with leaflets. Antiaircraft defenses blasted away, but the counterrevolutionists flew away and continued to battle Communism after their own fashion.[7]

"It was just a macho thing to do," Holloman commented, "and it gained a lot of support and hoopla, but it really wasn't accomplishing a damn thing except embarrassment to our government."[8]

The Cuban enclave was still abuzz with chatter of invasion and counterrevolution, and with the bitter laments of Batistianos seeking to reclaim their place in Cuba. Castro's counterintelligence forces tried to poison the nascent Miami exile community. There were distinct groups. In addition to the ex-Batista men, there were people who just plain hated Castro, and there were those who opposed Communism, period, Castro-led or not. They did share one common cause: scrubbing Cuba free of Fidel. But after that supposed three-prong invasion turned out to be a will-o'-the-wisp, talk of counterrevolution fell on cynical ears. And paranoia ran deep.

Which leads us to Colonel Morales Patino. A career officer in the Cuban navy, Patino had served under Batista and been imprisoned by Castro. By mid-June 1960, he surfaced in the Miami area. With the plan of recruiting a combat task force, Patino turned up about 150 men willing to be paid $75 a week to cover their families' expenses while they organized an army to battle Castro. The scheme sounded eerily familiar to many of those approached, and they listened to their better instincts. But there were others who couldn't commit to the mission fast enough. One man sold his car for eighty bucks to the first buyer who showed him the cash.[9]

An American hustler named Dave Hoffman was plucked out of a poolroom on June 11 when a Cuban crony, an ex-paratrooper named Raye Girarde, asked him if he wanted to pick up some dollars fighting Castro. Hoffman didn't have a hell of a lot else going on. The erstwhile cook figured, Why not? The promised rewards were tasty: a piece of land, a position in the proposed Cuban government, and best of all, his pick of the native women.[10] How could Hoffman lose?

He was next introduced to a Cuban called Richard, who brought him to a sign-up meeting at a Miami Springs house that served as the force's base of operation. Richard and Col. Patino were not working alone. There was American help. A Mr. Jones, who was tall and blond and wore a yellow shirt, explained it all to Mr. Hoffman. The men were headed for the mountains of Cuba where they would link up with seven or eight thousand more recruits, at that very moment being culled from all corners of the United States. Combat pay would be upped to $150 a week. Hoffman, whose military status was 4F (physically or mentally incapable of serving), lied and said he had army experience. He was sworn into the "Pan-American Confederation" and given a wallet card inscribed with the name of the organization.[11] Hoffman sat tight, dreaming dreams of counterrevolution.

Ricardo Jimenez Nunez was a Cuban cold warrior and the president of a group known by the Spanish acronym FACC, or Christian Anti-Communist Front. FACC's energies, like those of many groups in the Miami area, were devoted to disseminating propaganda against the Castro regime. But Jimenez Nunez's followers were far too excited by the idea of eradicating Fidel to let this opportunity pass, especially since the gathering army seemed to be in the good graces of the American government. Jimenez Nunez was suspicious, but he traveled to the Miami Springs home, which was owned by a Cuban named Ramon Crucet, to evaluate the details. Col. Patino, whom Jimenez Nunez had known in Cuba, assured him that the Pan-American Confederation did indeed have U.S. support. Patino was led to believe that an additional two or three thousand mercenaries from South America would join the Miami force at a training camp. Later, Jimenez Nunez brought a small group of his followers, which numbered about sixty, to the Miami Springs house for muster.[12]

"One day," he told Hal Hendrix, a reporter for the *Miami News,* "two Miami Springs policemen walked in and wanted to know what was going on. A Cuban American known to the men as 'Waldo' and one of the Americans explained it was a project being backed by the U.S." That was good enough for the credulous cops. They left.[13]

The Cuban American known as Richard picked up Dave Hoffman and Raye Girarde from a corner in downtown Miami on the evening of June 17. They were driven to the Miami Springs home once again. Mr. Jones assured them there was no cause for anxiety. The U. S. government, Jones said, echoing what recruits had been told all along, was behind this thing to the tune of 600 million dollars.[14]

Hoffman and others were shifted to a southwest Miami boarding house and put on ice. In the meantime, headquarters hit a series of snags.[15] Jimenez Nunez was ordered to have his would-be troops at the same boarding house at 9 A.M. on Monday, June 21. At about 9:30, Patino showed up and said he was holding a check that was so fat it couldn't be cashed. The men would have to reassemble later. At noon, they got another story, and a meeting was called at Crucet's house for 5 P.M.[16]

When the hour rolled around, Jimenez Nunez found about twenty cars parked near the house. He met with Patino, Crucet, Waldo, Jones, and the burly American in the yellow shirt who was called Phillip or Felipe. Waldo assured the men that everything was A-OK, revisiting the story about the check that was just too large to cash. Voices were raised.

"I said they would have to take the men out that night," Jimenez Nunez told Hal Hendrix. "Many other men were watching the operation to see if it was action or talk before joining."[17] At last, the leaders decided to move about sixty of them to Key Largo, where the men were transported by a convoy of automobiles.

"We passed several patrol cars riding down the highway and no one paid any attention to us. This made us think that all we had been told about U. S. support was true." They stopped driving when they reached the Rod and Reel Motel.

The group ran into problems with the motel's manager. He was suspicious about the men and their plans and Jimenez Nunez tried to allay his skepticism with a story about their being Cuban attorneys on a "convention holiday. He asked if we were mixed up in this Castro thing and I said we were just sightseeing."

Jimenez Nunez had been told the motel bill had been taken care of in advance. Not true. The manager was now looking for his money, and the men didn't have any. The red-fighter smelled a rat. "I called Crucet's house and was told by his wife that he and Patino and the others had left for Key Largo before noon. I called again and was told the number had been disconnected temporarily. The motel manager was threatening to call the sheriff."[18]

Dave Hoffman got to the Rod and Reel around midnight on Monday, June 20. He spent Tuesday afternoon poolside with his new buddies, Hoffman telling stories and lies and envisioning the glory that would soon be theirs.[19] Those in possession of more mature faculties, such as Jimenez Nunez, knew that they had been had. In addition to the Pan-American Confederation cards, the 60 soldiers of fortune had also been issued armbands with a white cross on it and the letters LL, which supposedly stood for the Legion of Liberty. "We really were being set up for a dandy trap. We were supposedly going to be flown into Cuba without any arms and identification cards and blue bands on our arms to make us quick targets."[20]

One recruit was allegedly waiting for a Mr. Smith to join Patino, Waldo, Felipe, and the others, but in the interregnum, Mr. Jones absconded with the payroll.[21] And the Tamale Squad was on its way. By 9:15 P.M. on June 22, when FBI agents led by Bob Dwyer arrived at the Rod and Reel, the Pan-American Confederation's rations consisted only of boxes of hardening, deep-fried pastry. Headline writers could not resist: the Doughnut Army was born.

Tamale Squad legend has it that Dwyer, standing alone behind a five-shot service revolver, apprehended all sixty recruits.[22] Jimenez Nunez remembered about six or eight G-men.[23] Special Agents Bill Kelly and Jack Barron were halfway to Key Largo that evening when word came over the radio that the situation at the Rod and Reel was under control. The pair were ordered back to Miami.[24]

FBI agents on the scene informed Jimenez Nunez and the others that they had been duped. They showed him a mug shot of Felipe, a known criminal, and word spread immediately throughout Cuban Miami that the whole misadventure was a Castro plot. Patino was acting in good faith, but Felipe, Jones, and the never-arrived Mr. Smith, if he ever existed, were American agents working for Castro. There was speculation that the whole thing was hatched by notorious mercenary Major William Morgan, an American who fought with Castro.[25] After the revolution took hold, Morgan had remained in Cuba to concentrate on counterespionage activities. During a classic Morgan scheme, the major persuaded an American pilot to land his aircraft on a piece of Havana highway. The pilot assumed he was picking up refugees bound for Miami, but instead was immediately surrounded by Castro troops. He was shot and his plane was destroyed. Some Cubans who had hoped to be flown to freedom were thrown in jail. Others were executed.[26]

These phony invasion plans, along with the alleged three-prong attack that was supposed to have been launched in January, were starting to acquire a hopeless familiarity. This was more misinformation and successful counterintelligence engineered by Castro's stateside agents. Felipe and Jones were rumored to be receiving a thousand bucks a head for each Cuban rounded up and brought back to Castro. Those in the know labeled the bizarre story of the Doughnut Army "another Morganaso."[27]

Dave Hoffman was never really aware of where he was going. He knew he was out of the Miami poolrooms he frequented, and he knew that he wasn't flipping any burgers or scrambling any eggs. That was all that seemed to matter to him. The *Miami Herald* ran him down a few days after the incident made the papers, and he told his story. Originally under the impression that he was being shipped to a training base in Jamaica, a wistful Hoffman told the reporter, "Man, I could just taste that rum and sunshine."[28]

6

THE CORAL
GABLES BOYS

In the early 1950s the CIA forged an identity as a lean, mean foreign policy machine. The agency was especially effective in the third world, which secretary of state John Foster Dulles shrewdly perceived to be the next battleground in the Cold War.[1] The agency's boys connected for the first time in Iran in 1953. When Iranian Premier Mohammed Mossadegh nationalized his country's oil industry and got too cozy with Iran's Communist Party, the CIA swung into action, papering Tehran with American money. The massive street demonstrations that the agency organized and paid for proved enough to topple Mossadegh. He was subsequently tossed in jail. The Shah was then brought out of exile and back to Iran, and the CIA wrangled changes in oil production that were favorable to western interests.[2]

"International Communism," Howard Hunt said, referring to the third world in a 2003 interview, "had been working for years to get a free hand in Central America." After a suspicious car accident took the life of his predecessor, the leftist leader Jacobo Arbenz, who had previously occupied a lesser government position, assumed power in Guatemala in 1951. He was, in Hunt's opinion, "a loyal and faithful servant of Stalin." Arbenz soon set about instituting "land reform," a policy that included the stealing back of 225,000 acres of United Fruit Company property. But United Fruit was a huge

American concern and an extremely well-connected one. The Washington lawyer Thomas "Tommy the Cork" Corcoran, acting in the interests of the firm, lobbied various congressmen and senators and brought them up to speed on the Guatemala situation.[3] In addition, DCI Dulles owned a batch of United Fruit stock, and so did his brother, John Foster. Foster had been (and Corcoran was) a partner at the powerhouse white-shoe law firm Sullivan and Cromwell, which represented United Fruit. And General Robert Cutler, National Security Council chairman, sat on United Fruit's board of directors.[4] Memo to the luckless Arbenz: It's a good idea to know who you're fucking with.

The CIA determined that Arbenz had to go. The political and military mechanisms of his overthrow were separated; Howard Hunt was drafted into service on the political side. His first order of business was vetting a successor to Arbenz. After a series of secret meetings with likely candidates, the agency, with Hunt's recommendation, settled on Colonel Carlos Castillo Armas, who had fled Guatemala and was living underground in New Orleans. "The decision having been made," Hunt said, "that Castillo was going to be the man, [the colonel] did his clandestine recruiting and [the CIA] provided transportation and training materials and did it in pretty rapid order. There was no point in fooling around. Arbenz was going to be defenestrated."

Redeploying the successful street agitation of Tehran, CIA operatives got Guatemalan wives and mothers out of their homes to bang pots and pans and laundry tubs in demonstrations against the Arbenz government.[5] The 1954 coup itself involved no American military personnel per se, although Eisenhower did authorize the use of some World War II vintage planes.[6] The aircraft made a few passes over Guatemala City and bombed an area in which civilian casualties would be unlikely but the mere sight of these planes was enough to terrorize the populace. The aircraft had been "sterilized and sanitized, so that nobody could trace them back to the CIA," Hunt said. "The people at state and the CIA headquarters were much more concerned with that than I was. I thought, you know, what the hell."[7] Arbenz got a strong feeling for which way the wind was blowing, and he got out of the country. The CIA had scored another hit.

The Guatemala action went so well that Arbenz's government collapsed in a week. During an after-action assessment at the Eisenhower White House, Ike wanted to know how many men Castillo Armas had lost in the operation. It turned out to be a grand total of one, a courier. The president was astonished. The agency brought him huge results by expending relatively little effort.[8]

In addition to the predictable diplomatic hand-wringing over these actions, decades after the fact, CIA has been accused of arrogance by many historians who have written about the period. It is doubtful that these critics ever plotted anything more complicated than a family vacation, but they make a fair point; on the other hand, it's tough to argue against the agency's ringing successes.

The CIA leaders had been together for a long time. Men of privilege and class, they shared glittering Ivy League backgrounds and a rock-solid belief in the righteousness of the United States, and were drawn, in large part, from Wild Bill Donovan's OSS. Richard Bissell, a graduate of Groton and Yale, did not fight with the armed forces during World War II. He served instead in a critical civilian role, focusing his brilliant (by every account) mathematical mind on the logistics of merchant shipping.[9] Bissell went to work full time at CIA in 1953, just in time for the Mossadegh overthrow, and although he was not a veteran of the OSS, by the time the

Dulles gang got revved up for their Cuban project, Bissell was in charge of all the agency's covert operations.

Bissell's deputy, Tracy Barnes, had been his classmate at Groton and Yale. Barnes was an immensely popular kid who grew into a man that nobody disliked. Bored with his Wall Street job, when the war broke out, he was drawn to the danger and excitement that the OSS offered. He was an absolute natural for CIA, and had played a key role in the Arbenz defenestration. Along with Jake Engler (Jacob Esterline's nom de guerre) the former CIA station chief in Venezuela, and a young Marine Corps colonel named Jack Hawkins, Bissell and Barnes were the main architects of the Cuba Project.

It is easy to understand why these veteran hands were so full of themselves during the first heady days of their Cuba Project. They must have felt like a championship team reassembled for another stab at glory. With Hunt in the game, and Tracy Barnes giving him direction, the men got ace radio propagandist Dave Phillips to go along for the ride, too. Why not? Phillips had also been a bang-up success in Guatemala. The information was highly classified, but everybody knew there was something in the air. When Engler approached Phillips to tell him what was up, he said, "I'll give you three guesses."

It didn't take Phillips long to come up with the right answers. He said, "Cuba. Cuba. And Cuba."[10]

Cuba. Cuba. And Cuba.

First things first. The Cuban people were going to need to be led by somebody or something once Castro was out of the way, and those leaders would have to come from somewhere. Enter Manuel "Manolo" Artime. The son of a Communist, Artime was a devout, Jesuit-educated Catholic who had taken a medical degree and was preparing for a career in psychiatry. A member of Castro's July 26 Movement, Manolo was working to help poor farmers improve their methods of cultivation, but he became almost immediately disenchanted with the Communist elements of Castro's government.[11] After he lashed out at Che Guevara and Raúl Castro, Artime's days in Cuba grew short.

He evaded a nationwide manhunt and was exfiltrated from his homeland by CIA operative (and Hunt's right-hand man) Bernard Barker, a Cuban national with an American father.[12] Barker managed to smuggle Artime aboard a freighter, and when the ship carrying him from Cuba docked in the bright morning sunshine in Tampa, Artime was met on the pier by a tall, white-haired American. He introduced himself as Mr. Burnett. Burnett gave Artime his first taste of the agency's cover story. He was in no way associated with the U.S. government. Instead, Burnett claimed, he was working for a consortium of capitalists who opposed Communism. They had friends in high places.[13]

But before Artime could be indoctrinated into the Cuba Project, the agency would have to vet him first. He was taken to Miami and holed up in a motel where he was interrogated, Rorschach-tested, and hooked up to a polygraph machine. Artime submitted to the process. How close was he to Castro, they wanted to know. Was Artime a Castro agent, or was he working for another government? What about his father? Had his father disavowed Communism? Had he done the same? His handlers came back late at night. Artime had passed their tests.

"From the beginning," Haynes Johnson wrote in *The Bay of Pigs*, "the Cuban counterrevolutionists viewed their new American friends with blind trust." Their options were limited of course, and though the naiveté of Artime and the others was fathered in some part by desperation, the Cubans believed in American power and in the very idea of America itself.[14]

Settling into Miami, Artime set up a group that opposed Castro, calling it the Movement of Revolutionary Recovery, or MRR. His group joined the dozens of other exile political organizations. Handsome, charismatic, young, and broke, Artime articulated with passion everything that was wrong with Castro's government. Hunt was very impressed after their first meeting. "He exuded," Hunt said, "the intangible charisma of leadership."[15]

Artime embarked on a CIA-sponsored speaking tour of Latin America, though he didn't know where the money was coming from. He was communicating by phone with a series of anonymous voices during this time, who, although they were always different men, used the same name. Artime received word that he should fly immediately to New York, check into the Statler Hilton, and await further instruction. It was, this contact said, vital to the future of Cuba. This was Manolo's first meeting with a man who called himself Frank Bender. "I was going to hear that name until the Bay of Pigs," Artime said. "Frank Bender. The Great Frank Bender."

Nobody mentioned the CIA or the U.S. government. The men discussed Artime's vision for the future of Cuba. Manolo was convinced that any return to a military dictatorship would doom the country to further Communist insurrections, and he outlined his ideas for achieving social justice in Cuba, taking special note of the interests of small farmers and land owners.

Artime articulated his plan for a guerrilla uprising in Oriente province. Bender pressed him. Why stop there? Artime explained that he didn't have the manpower or the firepower for an island-wide operation, and Bender responded that if Artime could bring him the bodies, Bender could get them the guns. They shook hands on the deal. This was Bender's parting shot: "Remember, Manolo, I am not a member of the United States government. I have nothing to do with the United States government. I am only working for a powerful company that wants to fight Communism."[16]

Naturally, Bender was lying, as Artime must have known, but he didn't have much of a choice except to go along for the ride. Bender (actually Gerry Droller) was an old CIA operative who had worked in Europe. He didn't know a peep of Spanish, and his manner, as that "Great Frank Bender" quote implies, was high-handed and clumsy. He clashed with the sophisticated, Spanish-fluent Hunt. Hunt felt that he outranked Bender; Bender saw things differently. Artime and other Cuban political leaders, who had by this time been culled from the swelling number of Miami exiles, basked in the glow of E. Howard's not inconsiderable charms. They hated the gruff Bender. Hunt saw Bender undoing all his hard work, and their distaste for one another got to such a point that Hunt got Bender banned from Miami.

Bender ignored him. He snuck into town to connect with a Cuban contact at an airport motel, and a woman who was occupying an adjoining room overheard their accents (Bender was Swiss-born) and their conversation. She turned out to be a secretary who recorded the details in shorthand; she also had a brother working for the FBI. She gave him her notes, and the bureau forwarded them to CIA. Bender got his wrist slapped; Hunt gloated.[17]

As word spread with the Cuban community that these so-called wealthy Americans were hatching a plot to overthrow Castro, recruitment for the Cuba Project, both political and military, got hot and heavy. Hunt, concentrating on winning political operatives for his new endeavor, had so much foot traffic in and out of his apartment, his neighbors suspected he was a bookmaker. A deal for another safe house went south because Howard couldn't convince the owner that he wasn't a gangster.[18]

Finally, he secured a residence in Coconut Grove. "Every night about ten or eleven o'clock Bernie Barker would come in and wake me in my bedroom," Hunt recalled. "I would go out and make the coffee or the liquor or whatever [the exile visitors] wanted. I would be up all night listening to the harangues and circumlocutions of these Cubans. The lady next door was the widow of a Pan American official. Our properties were separated by no more than thirty or forty inches. And she had a very nubile daughter who was just finishing a divorce." The neighbor attempted to fix up her daughter with the polished and erudite "bachelor." He said he wasn't interested, without letting on that he was already a married father. Her daughter thus rebuffed, and Hunt's all-night visitors being exclusively male, the neighbor reported to police that the house next door was a "nest of homosexuals," and that the head of the household could quite possibly be a gay pimp.[19]

The Cuba Project's top-secret Florida headquarters was set up in Coral Gables, home of the Biltmore Hotel and the University of Miami. Hunt was escorted to an office building that had been outfitted with sophisticated telecommunications gear and featured an extraordinary security presence. To deflect the natural curiosity such a site would attract, the agency concocted a cover story for the place: the building housed an electronics firm that held lucrative government contracts. For the short term, the story worked.[20]

On June 23, the same day the *Miami Herald* reported the misadventures of the Doughnut Army, the newspaper published a story announcing the formation of a new Cuban political movement. The Democratic Revolutionary Front, or the *Frente* in shortened Spanish, announced its existence and its intentions: the overthrow of Fidel Castro and the establishment of a provisional interim government. Datelined Mexico City, where the Frente had taken up headquarters, the story introduced to the world Dr. Manuel Artime, among others, who had agreed to fold his Movement of Revolutionary Recovery into the Frente. Since Artime's organization constituted only one wing of the Frente (the other members headed their own outfits), this rough alliance was going to need political management. That manager was E. Howard Hunt.

Shifting from Coral Gables and his Coconut Grove safe house to Mexico City, the peripatetic Hunt devised another cover story. In the Mexican capital, Howard was a novelist living off a fat inheritance. He brought his family with him. First order of business was touching base with "Sam," a CIA contact who rented a number of houses where the Frente could meet, and then got to work publishing a Frente organ called *Mambi*.[21]

Before he left for Mexico, Manuel Artime reached out to Jose Perez "Pepe" San Roman, a former career officer in the Cuban army, then living in Miami exile.[22] Along with other refugee professionals from the Cuban military, San Roman was spirited to a secluded island to undergo a series of American-administered tests. The men were supposed to have the impression that the U.S. government had nothing to do with this operation. CIA was using another cover story for military recruits—"a Cuban millionaire" was bankrolling their weapons, training, and housing. San Roman and the others were eventually transported to Panama, where they received training in guerrilla warfare. They stayed there for eight weeks.[23]

Another recruit, Erneido Oliva, had graduated officer training school in Cuba, but resigned his position in August 1959 and fled the country. "I was a lifelong Catholic," he said, "and I could not support Communism." Oliva was also recruited from the exile ranks in Miami. He was flown from Opa-Locka airport in North Miami to a location in Guatemala that stood in the shadow of an active volcano. It was obvious to Oliva—though when he asked the question, it was left hanging in the air—that the operation had the backing of the U.S. government.[24] The encampment, known as Base Trax, was going to be the launching pad for what the world would eventually know as the Bay of Pigs invasion.

Immediately after arriving, Oliva was reunited with several men he had served with in Cuba. On their first night together, the men prayed the rosary. They asked God to help them defeat Fidel Castro.[25]

A decision had been made to limit the force's ranks to between 800 and 900 men, but their serial numbers started at 2500. It was hoped that if word leaked back to Castro, he would assume that the army mounted against him numbered more than three times its actual total.[26] In September, a popular recruit named Carlos Rafael Santana was killed in a fall he suffered during a dangerous mountain-training mission. Santana's serial number was 2506—very low and denoting his early involvement—a fact that had always made Santana proud. This army in exile, in honor of their fallen comrade, christened their organization Brigade 2506.[27]

John F. Kennedy proved himself a tough campaigner. With his brother Robert twisting arms behind the scenes (he warded off a favorite-son run by Ohio governor Mike De Salle—whose support could then later be traded at the convention),[28] JFK, the celebrity candidate, racked up primary wins throughout the spring of 1960.

Kennedy ran hard against bitter opposition from Humphrey. Johnson's late-breaking candidacy and the (still) popular Stevenson's noncommittal stance represented fresh threats. And as late as July 10, the eve of the Democratic National Convention in Los Angeles, Kennedy, though confident, had cause for concern. His few lingering doubts were not misplaced. During the convention, Stevenson, "the sleeping candidate," awoke. "The explosion of enthusiasm for Stevenson," Robert Dallek wrote, "exceeded anything seen at a Democratic convention since William Jennings Bryan had gained the nomination on an emotional tide of protest in 1896."[29]

The Democratic Party, John F. Kennedy, and the American people were kept in suspense until the end of the states' roll call. When Wyoming pledged its fifteen votes to JFK, he took the nomination. After the usual Kennedy hardball calculations, Senate Majority Leader Lyndon Johnson of Texas, who had harbored his own ambitions, was named as his running mate.[30]

Richard Nixon, with Henry Cabot Lodge as his pick for vice president, emerged as the Republican presidential candidate at the end of July. The Republican National Convention lacked the drama and the heat that the Democrats generated, and the process was likened by some to a coronation.[31]

And so, by late July 1960, the Cuba Project enjoyed the full approval of the lame-duck Eisenhower administration, the enthusiastic support of the Republican presidential candidate, and the philosophical encouragement of the Democratic candidate, too. CIA had successfully recruited the political and military leaders of their clandestine operation against Fidel Castro. Their proposed provisional government had been established. The Miami exiles had plenty to be excited about. And as if all of this weren't quite convoluted enough, as summer wore on, other players had entered the fray with fresh ideas that deserved an airing.

For all of his erudition, Howard Hunt has been harshly criticized as something of an erratic performer. His own look back on this period, the 1973 book *Give Us This Day*, relates with candor the nightmare of trying to put together anything like a united Cuban government in exile. Hunt had submitted his own four-point plan on the Cuba Project, and he was of a mind with other government officials on at least one course of action: bump off one or another of the Castro brothers, or both.[32] The higher-ups at Dulles's CIA had the vision, the means, and the balls to try it.

In July of 1960, a volunteer operative in Cuba reached out to the agency, reporting that he was about to come into close contact with Raúl Castro. Officials got back to him the next day, asking through the Havana station if this Cuban would be interested in taking extreme action against Raul. The idea was to "arrange an accident" that might be fatal to Raúl. Evidently the man agreed, but upon further reflection, and after the Havana contact had already been set in motion, word came through from Washington to abort the mission. Luckily for the operative who planned it, he never got close enough to Raúl to make it happen.

Putting Raúl on a shelf, the agency pursued a number of less realistic schemes to humiliate Fidel on his home turf. One idea had CIA "assets" contaminating the location from which Castro beamed out one of his rambling trademark soliloquies with an LSD-type substance, causing Fidel to spout some hoped-for, delusional mumbo jumbo that would befuddle the populace. Another plot had operatives treating his shoes with thallium salts, a powerful depilatory, the theory being that as the fumes wafted north from his footwear, the chemical would strip the leader of his beard, and Samson like, deprive him of his charisma and strength. Yet another plan was to poison a box of Castro's cigars with a strain of botulism so overwhelming, Castro would drop dead the second the tobacco tube touched his lips. No word on whether or not the stogies ever found their way to Fidel.[33]

Richard Bissell, the agency's covert operations head, was having his patience worn thin with these misfires. In August, Bissell was approached by Sheffield Edwards, a highly motivated and coldly efficient agency man. At Bissell's office the two brainstormed plans to kill Fidel, but Edwards had arrived with an idea: why not contract the mob to do the hit? La Cosa Nostra had the experience and the means, and best of all, the motive. Fidel's nationalization program had turned the Havana casinos into empty hulks, draining, literally, millions of dollars from gangland coffers. Bissell gave Edwards the green light.[34]

One of the first challenges facing CIA brass was to create and maintain plausible deniability. They handed the kill-Castro job to Jim O'Connell, the operations chief of the agency's security division. "Big Jim" was an ex-FBI man with a strong track record of dirty business and a "hands-on approach," but the team needed another link in the chain to further distance the matter from their official government agency. Big Jim knew just who to call: Robert Maheu.[35]

Maheu, like O'Connell, was an ex-Hooverite who was then operating in Washington, D.C., as a private investigator. Heading his client list was Howard Hughes[36]—California industrialist, aviator, defense contractor, and, by that time, all-around weirdo. Maheu had also been dirty enough for long enough to become well acquainted with one Johnny Rosselli.

In the 1920s while still a teenager, an Italian immigrant named Filippo Sacco beat it out of the tough Boston neighborhood where a series of criminal charges hung over his head.[37] He got lost for a time in New York, then went west to hook up with the expanding Chicago mob of Al Capone.[38] It was Capone who insisted that he adopt the Italian a.k.a. (Filippo had been using a generic WASP-y alias), and the world knew him from 1923 onward as Johnny Rosselli.[39]

Rosselli moved to Los Angeles that same year after a physician diagnosed an early mutation of TB. He prospered in the rackets, eventually hooking up with the Jack Dragna gang.[40] It was here in the city of countless manufactured mirages, of infinite self-inventions and reinventions, that Filippo Sacco truly remade himself into Johnny Rosselli. He got rid of his ghetto accent, dressed in custom clothes, and became something of a wine connoisseur. "This penchant for etiquette was unusual in a street thug," the Rosselli biographers Charles Rappeleye and Ed Becker wrote in *All American Mafioso: The Johnny Rosselli Story*. "[These characteristics] would come to distinguish Rosselli from most of his underworld colleagues."[41]

Johnny flourished in the wide-open Los Angeles of the 1930s. He smoothed out turf battles and ironed out the wrinkles caused by pint-sized gangster and New York transplant Mickey Cohen, then on the rise. And he provided entrée and contacts to another ascendant Jew from the east, Benjamin "Bugsy" Siegel.[42]

After a wartime army stint during which he saw no combat and after serving a prison bid for labor racketeering, Johnny returned to Los Angeles. Still on parole, he could only meet clandestinely with mob associates like Jack Dragna and the Cleveland import Jimmy "The Weasel" Frattiano at his lawyer's office. Frattiano, who was slugging it out on the streets of L.A., took credit for the murders of Tommy Trombino and Dominic Brancata in the bloody Sunset Strip gang war with Mickey Cohen. Clearly, there were a lot of idiots running around the City of Angels during the late 1940s and early 1950s. But "if Johnny Rosselli woulda became the boss," The Weasel said, "they woulda all been millionaires in Los Angeles."[43]

If Rosselli felt slighted by his being passed over for boss of the L.A. rackets, he didn't let it interfere with his wheeling and dealing. And if he had been made boss, it would have been as head of a very weak family. It appears that he was content to be exactly who he was. "Johnny was just a soldier," Frattiano said, "but they respected him for the simple reason that he was smart. Jack [Dragna] would make no moves without talking to Johnny."[44]

Rosselli thrust his now silver-maned self into the booming breach of 1950s Las Vegas. By that time, his reputation as a mob fixer was legendary, and he glided among various organized crime factions in "open cities," that is, territories—such as Miami—not controlled by a single crime family. He eventually touched down in the gangster's paradise that Havana had become during Batista's second iteration as president.[45]

By the time the plot to hit Castro gained traction, Bob Maheu was so tight with Johnny Rosselli that Rosselli had once enjoyed a Thanksgiving dinner at Maheu's home.[46] Big Jim O'Connell debriefed Maheu on the agency's cover line, that is, *Maheu* was now supposed to pass himself off as the agent of businessmen with Cuban investments. They wanted Castro out of the way, the story went, so that they could recover some of the cash that they had sunk into the country.[47]

But Maheu had a lot of confidence in Johnny, and rather than insult his mob buddy with bullshit about businessmen,

Maheu told him the truth. They had their first sit-down at the Brown Derby restaurant in Los Angeles in the late summer of 1960.[48] Rosselli refused to do it for the money. Sharpie, fixer, and would-be infantryman, Johnny Rosselli shared the patriotic sentiments of his fellow gangster Meyer Lansky. He agreed to take the job for the love of his country.[49] With the United Nations General Assembly looming, and with the Cuban leader's New York arrival imminent, Maheu and Rosselli talked about the best way to whack Fidel Castro.[50]

What might have stood had they not fallen. JFK receives the ransomed leaders of Brigade 2506, Palm Beach, December, 1962. Left to right: Unidentified man, Roberto Perez San Roman, Jose Perez "Pepe" San Roman, the President, Manuel Artime, Erneido Oliva, and Enrique Ruiz Williams. Appears by permission of the Associated Press.

The Tamale Squad, circa 1960. Left to right: Davis, Pedregon (translator), Holloman, Dwyer, Albaugh, Edmiston, Kelly, Hayes, Errion, Stafford. Image first appeared in The Investigator, *FBI in-house publication.*

Detectives perp walk The Hook. Note cigarette in remaining hand, cuffed to cop. Appears by permission of the Associated Press.

The Hook, in hat, with friends. Appears courtesy of Bill Kelly.

Bette noir: Molina associate (and Bill Kelly antagonist) Jorge Antonio Rodriguez Orihuela. Appears courtesy of Bill Kelly.

Our Men in Havana: FBI Special Agents and eventual Tamale Squad members Edwin Sweet (left) and William Friedemann. After their diplomatic cover was blown in Havana, the Castro government charged them with "counterrevolution" and expelled them from Cuba. Appears courtesy of Bill Kelly.

Bill "Machine Gun" Kelly at the FBI's training facility in Quantico, Va., early 50s. Note absence of trademark drum magazine in General Thompson's invention. The gun isn't loaded. Appears courtesy of Bill Kelly.

Artist's rendering of the Hotel Nacional, Havana, mid-1950s. Appears courtesy of the Author.

From Jane to Dot with a caveat. The reverse reads, "If you want to lose your bankroll fast, this is the spot." Appears courtesy of the Author.

The insignia of Brigade 2506 as it appears on a sleeve patch. Courtesy of the Author.

(opposite) The erudite E. Howard Hunt. His trials as the CIA's political liaison to Brigade 2506 were eclipsed by later infamy during the Watergate scandal. For his role in that caper, he served three years in federal prison. Photo appears courtesy of the Associated Press.

The gangster side. George Raft proves there is life after movie stardom, propped against a gaming table in the late 50s. Appears courtesy of Time Life Pictures / Getty Images.

The Lions in Winter. Bill Kelly, left, and Howard Hunt in Hunt's South Florida home, December, 2003. Appears courtesy of the Author.

7

THE HOOK

On September 19, 1960, with the United Nations General Assembly set to kick off, Soviet leader Nikita Khrushchev and his delegation steamed into New York harbor aboard the good ship *Baltika*. The International Longshoremen's Union had dispatched a welcoming party, and its members took the trouble to prepare some written greetings. "Roses are red, violets are blue" one pithy placard quipped, "Stalin dropped dead, How about you?" Less poetic but more to the point, another sign read "Dear K! Drop dead you bum!"[1] The tone on the street had been set.

Diplomatic luminaries were housed all over town, each with his own security contingent; with the New York Police Department and other law enforcement agencies deployed to keep the peace, the General Assembly was a twenty-four-hour security headache. Khrushchev bounced between the Soviet mission on Park Avenue and an estate on Long Island. He seemed to be everywhere at once, even popping up on David Susskind's TV show.[2] It remains unclear what his rolling press conferences and appearances at various soirées were supposed to accomplish, but he overstayed his welcome.

Khrushchev was the very personification of the Soviet bear. "Crude, unpredictable, occasionally violent," David Halberstam wrote, "Khrushchev seemed to be the embodiment of the sheer animal force of the Soviet Union."[3] His behavior was boorish even by the standards of a Russian peasant. Though he had indulged in some random fist-banging during UN meetings that didn't proceed to his liking, the Soviet leader outdid himself on October 11, his last full day in New York. The incident went down as the defining moment of the 1960 General Assembly.

After he gave a talk and was returning to his place, Khrushchev noticed that Spanish representatives weren't responding in the way he thought they should.[4] When he got to his seat, he slipped off his loafer and began to bang it on the table. Andrei Gromyko, his foreign minister, was seated next to him; he blanched.

"With a 'grimace of determination and the look of a man about to plunge into a pool of icy water,'" Khrushchev biographer William Taubman wrote, quoting Nikita's son, "'the foreign minister removed his shoe and began tapping it gently on the desktop as if hoping his boss would notice but no one else would.'"

Most of the other Communists in attendance, including those from the Soviet Union, were mortified. Khrushchev, for his part, said he was just trying to liven up the proceedings. Back home in Moscow a few days later, he declared victory.[5]

Fidel Castro's second U.S. visit drew a different reaction than his East Coast laurel run seventeen months earlier. Havana's shrill tone was matched by Washington's. Neither side seemed much interested in diplomacy, and the press spurred along this parting of the ways with glee.

Castro's first public relations problem came when his contingent got bounced from the Shelburne Hotel on Lexington Avenue. Some of the Cubans, relatively fresh from mountain maneuvers, treated the hotel like they were still on bivouac. There were reports of the contingent traveling with live poultry, and one witness recalled that the men were actually roasting chickens in the hotel's hallways. The delegation was forced to relocate to the Hotel Theresa, at 125th Street and Seventh Avenue, where a Theresa official said the guests behaved like perfect gentlemen.[6]

The scene outside the hotel was less sanguine. The NYPD steered pro- and anti-Castro demonstrators behind barricades erected on opposite sides of the street, a neutral zone of a block or so between them.[7] Cops were forced to add an additional seventy-five officers to their security detail, bringing the number to over three hundred[8] after Khrushchev ventured uptown for an impromptu bear hug with Castro.[9]

Not long before, Kevin Tierney had been conscripted to the army's Counter Intelligence Corps, or CIC. Bronx born and Catholic educated, Tierney had graduated from Bishop Stepinac High in White Plains,[10] an institution named for the Croatian cleric that Yugoslavian strongman Josef Tito had murdered in 1946.[11] The archdiocese of New York intended the school's name to be a reminder of the global struggle against Communism, and although Tierney's indoctrination as a cold warrior began with his attendance at Stepinac, it did not end there. By 1960, his school days were behind him but his politics remained staunchly anti-Communist.

Tierney and his counterparts from navy and air force intelligence divided their time between the Russian consulate and the Hotel Theresa. There was nothing covert about their operation. Up on 125th Street, Tierney said to an officer, "Do you see something wrong with this picture? We're the only white guys [wearing] suits and short haircuts. Don't you think they know who we are?" He was told to shut up and do his job.

The barricades to control protestors were a safety measure, but Tierney and his team combed the neighborhood looking for signs of suspicious activity and characters. "Now," Tierney said, "they call it profiling."

His assignment took him to a coffee shop on 130th and Lenox Avenue, where voices had been raised for and against Castro since the Cuban leader's arrival in New York. Though the passions were evident, the intelligence men did not become involved in politics. With their short hair and their suits and their whiteness, they were there to provide a physical presence, a reminder to partisans of all stripes that their activities were not being ignored; somebody was watching. "We just wanted to keep the situation cool until we could get this goddamn guy the hell out of the country."

Army CIC took a back-up role to street cops in keeping pro- and anti-Castro forces from each other's throats, preventing the possibility of an all-out Harlem riot, and making sure no Castro haters got into the Theresa. But within the Cuban diplomatic corps, individuals lingered who did not approve of the direction in which their government was going, unbeknownst to Castro. It was Tierney's responsibility to make sure they remained unidentified. Exposure might cost them their lives. These men had reached out to CIC.

Law enforcement and intelligence were keenly aware of the physical threats against Castro. "But no matter what was going on down in Cuba, he was not going to be assassinated on U.S. territory." Tierney's orders were clear. He was told explicitly, "What they do in Cuba is their business. He can't be killed up here.

"You're telling me I gotta take a bullet," Tierney mused, "to keep that son of a bitch alive so he can go back down to Cuba and have them kill him?"

Tierney was told he had it right.[12] On Seventh Avenue and 125th Street, Fidel Castro stayed alive, but not because the myriad intelligence and law enforcement agencies were competing with one another to keep him safe. United States soil, by law, was supposed to be off limits to the CIA. That was one advantage Tierney and his CIC colleagues had over the agency, as he pointed out in an interview. But of course, there *were* agency men in New York during the time of the United Nations General Assembly. Some had set up a suite at the Waldorf-Astoria to entertain NYPD men assigned to keep Castro unharmed. A CIA operative breezily informed a member of police brass about his intentions of getting an exploding cigar into Castro's mouth. If all went well, it should take Fidel's head clean off. Apparently, the agency man wasn't joking, but if he was, the cop was far from amused.[13]

Antagonists of the American government were busy, too. An odd piece of intelligence ephemera points to Communist agitation from the period. A CIA field memo hacked out on Park Chambers hotel stationery details an interview conducted with one Richard Gibson. The memo is undated and unsigned, but the report's references to events clearly indicate that the debriefing took place in the autumn of 1960. Gibson was a "Negro," in the parlance of the day, a radical, and a Communist sympathizer. He also liked his scotch. The agency operative cracked a fifth the second the man sat down, and Gibson helped himself for the next four hours. The whiskey loosened his tongue.

Gibson hated America. He insisted that all black people did. They took delight in the American losses during the Korean War, but the irony that black soldiers died in Korea seemed to be lost on him. "He made it very clear," the report states, "that he is very much committed to the stirring up of the Negroes, to make trouble, almost any kind of trouble."

Gibson was entwined with a Castro-sponsored front known as the Fair Play for Cuba Committee, and he told the reporter that the committee received "$1,500 each issue or monthly" from the Cuban government for publishing a newsletter. As the night wore on and Gibson's scotch intake mounted, his ramblings became more sensational. He claimed to have told Castro that for $2,000 he could get two thousand American students down to Cuba for the Christmas season, provided the Cuban government picked up their air fare and lodging. Gibson thought this would be a marvelous propaganda victory for Fidel: a couple thousand American college kids extolling the virtues of his leftist government.

"This fellow Gibson definitely doesn't care a whit about Cuba," the reporter concludes. "He is interested in using Cuba for just as much as Cuba is worth as a headache for the U.S. He literally said that. And his other remarks convinced me that what he wants is trouble, trouble, trouble for the U.S. His theme apparently is the Negro defiance theme. Very destructive."[14]

On Eighth Avenue near 51st Street, El Prado was way across town from the Turtle Bay headquarters of the UN and seventy-four blocks south of the Hotel Theresa. A bar and grill that specialized in Spanish cuisine, the place was a popular hangout for the Latin crowd. It was after three o'-clock. The rush was over and a barmaid named Rosa Morales was relaxing over lunch with a friend.[15]

A group of Castro sympathizers, some sporting the red and black of July 26, were digesting their midday meals. In walked a handful of men from an outfit opposed to Fidel's brand of leadership, a group known as the Cuban Front, or the Democratic Revolutionary Movement. They had called ahead for an order of sandwiches, fortifications for anti-

Castro pickets walking the line at the Theresa. Front members were recognized by the July 26ers. A pro-Castro man slipped away and returned a few minutes later with some friends.[16]

"*Vete,*" he told Rosa Morales.

Rosa kept eating.

"*Vete de aqui,*" the man repeated, stronger this time. Get out of here. Rosa left the table and went outside.[17]

The July 26ers, whose numbers had been reinforced to at least twelve, surrounded the five men of the Cuban Front. Insults shot back and forth. Somebody said something about the United States being a free country while Cuba was in chains. A beer bottle smashed against a wall. Fists flew. Furniture went flying. Chairs were busted up, and high over the scrum, a lean arm with a metal appendage went up and came down, each time on top of an anti-Castro skull. Shrieks of pain echoed through the barroom. Then a shot rang out. And another shot.[18]

Front member Louis Rodriguez caught a bullet in the shoulder. Two other men with head wounds sprawled out where they fell, and customers went screaming into the street. Police sirens wailed closer. The fight broke up but one patron wasn't moving. Nine-year-old Magdalena Urdaneta, on vacation from Venezuela, lay slumped in her mother's arms, a .38 caliber slug lodged in her stomach.[19]

Cops arrived to find El Prado nearly deserted and the people who had stuck around weren't too helpful. Witnesses did agree on one thing, though. The man with the gun was the same man who wore a metal prosthesis where his right hand once was,[20] and he was the same guy who told Rosa Morales to beat it. She knew him as Pancho.[21] Others called him El Gancho: The Hook.

The beaten and injured were transported to St. Clare's Hospital. Humberto Triana, who tasted The Hook's sting, was treated and released. Francisco Pereira took a few stitches in the scalp before doctors told him he could go home, and Louis Rodriguez, a bullet having passed clean through his shoulder, received the attention he needed and would soon recover. Little Magdalena was grievously wounded and was immediately operated on when she got to the hospital.[22]

Already jittery with the strain of protecting all those visiting diplomats, NYPD units were ordered to be doubly aware of the threat of further violence between opposing Castro groups. After police determined that the man with the hook was the shooter, they dispatched teletypes describing Francisco Molina to every law enforcement agency in the city. Gunsmiths and pawnshops were told to be leery of anybody trying to unload a .38 caliber automatic.[23] It was a start.

Frank Weber, the cop who had arrested John Gregory Feller with his homemade bomb in 1959, was called in to investigate this crime, too. The 16th Detective Squad was on the El Prado scene early, and after he had gotten what he could from the people who were still hanging around, Weber attempted to bring definition to the shadows that formed out of the sketchy, preliminary details. He canvassed the rooming houses and the stark tenements that stood thick on the ground west of Times Square. He asked questions. Molina was no stranger in the Cuban community, and Weber was able to build a background based on the answers he got.[24]

His full name was Francisco Molina del Rio and he was born in Havana on April 1, 1932. He immigrated to the United States in the early 1950s and found work as a machine operator in a factory that made tiles. An accident on that job cost him his right hand. Returning to Cuba, Molina found a slot with the Havana police during the last dark days of

Batista rule. Then, in late 1959, he reentered the United States for the specific purpose of intimidating stateside Cubans who opposed Castro. Since his accident, Molina wore a hook over the stump where his right hand had been, or when the spirit moved him and his skull-cracking services weren't required, a primitive prosthetic hand.[25]

Weber kept asking questions. One answer led to an address, and a reply at that place took him to another building, until he found himself standing in front of an apartment house on 57th Street. The super knew who Weber was talking about, and told him that Molina lived upstairs but wasn't home. Molina's residence was staked out,[26] but The Hook wasn't coming home any time soon.

On the morning of September 22, 1960, Magdalena Urdaneta took a turn for the very worst. Doctors fought to save her, but at six o'clock the little girl slipped away.[27] Her parents, whose lives would never be the same from that day forward, flew home to Caracas to lay their baby to her final rest.[28]

A tremendous outpouring of sympathy followed the family home. The American ambassador to the United Nations, James J. Wadsworth, issued a statement saying " . . . I wish to extend my sympathy to Venezuela and specially to the bereaved parents. I feel all the more keenly about this because Magdalena was the innocent victim of a completely senseless and unnecessary act by hoodlums who showed disregard for the rights of others."[29]

Francis Cardinal Spellman, head of the New York archdiocese, celebrated a special mass for Magdalena. "I accompany you," the cardinal wrote in a telegram to her mother and father, "in your profound sorrow."[30]

Anti-Castro protestors rimmed their placards in black in memoriam of the nine-year-old's tragic death, and a group calling itself the Anti-Castro Front wasted no time blaming the dictator for Magdalena's death, calling her "the innocent victim of a blood-hungry tyrant."[31]

Though he was far from the action, Castro himself had a different take on the incident. After a party at the Theresa thrown by CIA informant Gibson's Fair Play for Cuba Committee, Castro told reporters that his opponents were responsible for the tragedy. He accused the American newspapers of making up lies and said, "Enemies of the revolution [fired the shot]."[32]

Law enforcement fired a few verbal shots back. They believed that if Castro was aware of Molina's political ties, he might well be able to help them in their investigation. They urged him to come forward. The Beard demurred.

The Molina manhunt intensified. Frank Weber partnered with Ed Larkin of Manhattan West Homicide, a cop with thirty-one years on the job.[33] Julio Hernandez, then living in Brooklyn but Cuban-born, was busted for felonious assault when Francisco Pereira put him at El Prado among the Castro agitators. One lead went instantly cold when cops grabbed a man with an amputated right hand at Idlewild airport, but he turned out to be a Queens resident who was at the airport to pick up his wife.[34]

As the case developed a deepening political chiaroscuro, the FBI's New York office related details of the investigation to J. Edgar Hoover. Fearing that he would cross state lines to avoid prosecution, Hoover had an arrest warrant issued for Molina. The Hook was now a federal fugitive, and there was an even greater possibility that he would attempt to flee the country. Hoover called The Hook the leader of a "goon squad" of Fidelistas, and added, with some satisfaction, that the man was "a known marihuana peddler."[35]

All fifty-four FBI field offices were put on alert, and the director dispatched hundreds of G-men to airports and steamship offices, to train terminals and car rental companies, to prevent Molina from slipping out of U.S. territory. Naturally, the Miami area received special attention. Hoover demanded that every flight bound for Cuba or Latin America be checked twice by his agents, personally.

To Bill Kelly and the Tamale Squad, it sounded like Mr. Hoover was trying to bottle up the United States by whatever means necessary. Kelly and a colleague named Bliss were posted at the Miami airport, keeping an eye peeled for Air Cubana flights to Havana, and here they caught a break: Cubana was reduced to two Havana-bound flights a day. During one of their ten-hour shifts, Bliss mentioned that he'd seen a newspaper advertising cheap air conditioners, and Bliss needed one. It was September, high summer in Miami, and Bliss and his wife were broiling. But Bliss had to get to the store by five. Kelly told him he could cover the remainder of the tour alone.

Ticket holders filed down the walkway and got into their seats. Kelly boarded the plane to get a look at the passengers, checking their faces against photographs of Molina and a known associate, a tiny snapshot that had been squeezed off during a May Day parade some years before. Neither man was on that flight.

Kelly was about to head back through the concourse. The Vickers prop plane revved its engines and appeared moments from takeoff, except that nobody had yet bothered to close the door. Kelly spotted a steward in the open doorway, waving his arms. He checked his pictures again. Three men were making a break for the plane. In the middle was the guy from the May Day parade. Kelly punched him in midstride.

The man went down, but his compatriots continued their dash for that open door.

Working Customs was an agent named Brown. "Brownie," Kelly hollered, "grab those two!" Brown apprehended both men and led them to a Customs office, along with Mr. May Day Parade, who turned out to be Francisco Molina's known associate, Jorge Antonio Rodriguez Orihuela. The three men were Cuban nationals, but they were all traveling on Canadian passports. The agents pulled fourteen pieces of luggage off the plane that belonged to the party. Kelly and Brown sorted through the bags.

They uncovered a membership list, money earmarked for the July 26 Movement, and a sealed manila envelope from the Cuban consulate in New York.

Brown started to unseal the envelope. Rodriguez Orihuela rushed him and suffered his second knockdown. Inside the envelope the agents found a typed radio address that condemned the United States air force for its treatment of Cuban nationals who served with them. There was also a military ID inside. It belonged to one of the other men, who turned out to be an American air force deserter, and he, it appeared, was going to give the radio address himself.

All three men were arrested. J. Edgar Hoover was so pleased with Kelly's work that he awarded the agent a special commendation and a two-hundred-dollar bonus. Rodriguez Orihuela, softened up by that pair of knockdowns, was smiling and chatty with Kelly and Brown, no hard feelings. He didn't give them anything on Francisco The Hook Molina.[36]

Three weeks later The Hook was still at large. The one-hundred-member task force of detectives and FBI men was broken up, with only Weber and Ed Larkin remaining on the case. Weber ran down one lead that took him to a house painter named Gustavo Romeau. During the course of their investigation, cops interviewed dozens of people who knew Molina, but none had seen him recently. The Hook's background got filled out, with details on the 1955 accident that had taken off his right hand, his time with the Havana cops, and his reentry to the United States popping up again and again. But Weber wasn't getting any closer to the man. Romeau stayed elusive as well, and as the painter got tougher to find, Weber got more interested. He started questioning contractors. Romeau's listed residences got closer to the present date. Then Weber connected with a man who had used him on a job just a few weeks before.

October 14 fell on a Friday in 1960. Ed Larkin was in court that morning testifying in another case, so Frank Weber grabbed a pair of FBI agents and drove through rush hour traffic to the address he had for Gustavo Romeau. It was in Queens.[37] A good-looking brunette answered the buzzer at the Sunnyside apartment, looking like she was on her way to work. The door swung open on a man in his underwear, sitting on the couch. He matched the description of Gustavo Romeau, and when cops asked, he said yes, he was their guy.[38] Romeau and the woman admitted they knew Francisco but couldn't help with his whereabouts. Weber noticed a pair of trousers slung over a chair back. Sifting through the pockets, he pulled out a green card. It belonged to Francisco Molina del Rio.[39]

Weber went room to room, throwing back drapes and pulling open doors. He walked into a bedroom gun first and found himself staring at a closed closet door. He threw it open on a rack of dresses, and pushing the garments aside, he saw a crouching man clad in pajama bottoms. They locked eyes.[40]

Weber said, "Come on out."

The man emerged, a stump where his right hand used to be.

"You're The Hook."

"No. I'm Francisco Molina del Rio."

Weber told him to get dressed. Molina fixed a prosthetic hand over his stump, and along with Romeau and Annie Ward, the attractive brunette who had leased the apartment, was transported to the West 54th Street station house. The three were arraigned before General Sessions Judge Mitchell Schweitzer. Molina was held without bond for the killing of Magdalena Urdaneta, and Romeau and Ward were remanded as material witnesses on bonds of twenty-five thousand dollars.[41]

Cops went at The Hook hard. He was questioned by the head of the DA's Homicide Bureau, Alexander Herman. Molina denied firing the shot that killed Magdalena, but he did place himself at El Prado during the brawl. Somebody else, The Hook said, did the shooting. Not me.[42] He had gone into hiding after the fight, and claimed that he had been sleeping in Central Park for the past three weeks, a story the police weren't buying. But he did say that as they were closing in on him, The Hook considered surrendering. He was exhausted and he was beaten and he knew it.[43]

This much of his story rings true. With the New York papers blanketing the story, Molina's 54th Street perp-walk was flashbulbed into infinity. The snapshots expose him for the hunted man he was, dark eyes rimmed in raccoon black, his mouth hanging open more in terror than in denial. Weber and another cop stand grim sentry on either side of him, Molina's prosthetic fingers curled stiffly at his waist.

Fair Play for Cuba troublemaker Richard Gibson, according to that CIA field memo written from the Park Chambers hotel, had advised the Cubans to get Molina out of town immediately after the shooting. "And then the stupid fellow was caught right here in the New York area." Against the backdrop of ongoing drama at the UN General Assembly, Gibson's comments on the El Prado incident suggest the brawl was a planned attack on anti-Castro Cubans. "Sometimes," Gibson muttered cryptically, "you have to eliminate someone."[44] But if Gibson thought "eliminating" a nine year-old kid did anything to help anybody's cause, there was a lot more wrong with him than a bellyful of scotch.

Police Commissioner Stephen Kennedy commandeered the subsequent press conference, obliged to dodge the political questions. He was not, he reminded reporters, there to make any statements on the international ramifications of the murder. But he did note that the brawl was waged between men wearing buttons that said "Castro and Khrushchev go home" and The Hook's gang of thugs, some wearing berets with the insignia of Castro's July 26 Movement.[45]

The same day that The Hook's pallor was further whitened by flashing cameras, the *Daily News* published a tiny item reporting that NYPD protocol was returning to where it stood before the UN General Assembly began.[46] The security belt was unknotted. Cops drifted back to their normal posts. Frank Weber was promoted from third to second grade detective. Nikita Khrushchev and Fidel Castro were safe at home.

There was no published reaction from the family of Magdalena Urdaneta.

8

POLITICS AND OTHER MEANS

Although Eisenhower had advised him against it, Richard Nixon agreed to a series of debates with John F. Kennedy. Nixon loved a fight, and, as Kennedy biographer Robert Dallek has pointed out, he was no stranger to the ascendant medium of television. His "Checkers speech" in 1952 (during which he responded to allegations that he had taken illegal gifts) was the "most successful use of television by an American politician to date." John F. Kennedy was about to change all that.

The first Kennedy-Nixon debate was staged in Chicago on September 26, 1960. Kennedy, the candidate for whom the phrase "tanned, rested, and ready" was coined, capitalized on his relaxed manner by aiming his opening statement right into the TV lens. He directly addressed the American voter. He appeared the very model of youthful vigor, good looks, and, in spite of ongoing health battles, vitality. Nixon looked sick. In fact, he wasn't completely recovered from an infection he developed over an old knee injury. His handlers had applied a coat of shaving powder over his ever-present five-o'clock shadow, and under the blazing glare of the television lights, Nixon, a man who was sensitive to heat, began to sweat profusely. He looked as if he were about to dissolve before American voters.[1]

History, as everybody knows, belongs to the victor, and on that particular evening the image of JFK demolished the image of Dick Nixon. Television as a means (and as an end) in campaigning dealt a knockout blow to all other media and to personal appearances, which thereafter began to be staged for TV. American politics changed forever. Television, with its unrelenting, reductive nature, had changed it.

On the same October Saturday in 1960 that the New York tabloids were saturated with the capture of Pancho-El Gancho, a quieter story lay buried on the inner pages. In a stump speech Senator Lyndon B. Johnson delivered to the New Orleans Press Club the day before, Johnson had sketched a plan to interrupt what he called "massive Communist penetration of Latin America." The arm-twisting Texas Democrat, now John F. Kennedy's running mate, called the situation in Cuba "a mess."

The vice presidential nominee and Lone Star pit bull pounded the Republicans again in another speech, while his campaign bus, the LBJ Special, was idling in a parking lot. He claimed that the global standing of the United States had plummeted to an all-time low, and that the country had to own up to the fact that "our defenses are down, our leadership is under attack, and our people are in need."[2]

The consummate politico, LBJ was right on message, and his charges were nothing new to anybody with even the faintest interest in the campaign. During the early cold war years, it was Republicans who made the political hay with the "red menace," although it was Truman, the Democrat, who had committed troops to Korea. Peace came to the peninsula under Eisenhower, but after the noise died down, it was the Democrats and their liberal leaders who were perceived to be "soft" on Communism. By the time the 1960 presidential campaign rolled around, the Dems were adamant: they vowed not to be seen as ambivalent toward the reds. Democrats were itching for an issue that showed not only that they were tough, but tougher than the Republicans.[3] Fidel Castro handed them the fight on a silver platter.

Jack Kennedy pumped up the body Democrat for a muscular pose-down against the Republicans. Under Eisenhower defense budget cuts, the country had become vulnerable. The Democrats hammered home the idea of a "missile gap" (there was none) and took every chance to harangue the Republicans on Cuba.[4]

Kennedy realized that the electorate's cold war jitters were more connected to what was happening in the northern Caribbean than to anything going on in Eastern Europe. As if Americans needed reminding, Kennedy pounded home the fact that Cuba was practically swimming distance from Key West, Florida. He couldn't make the point often enough. An October speech in Pennsylvania was typical. "Mr. Nixon hasn't mentioned Cuba very prominently in this campaign. He talks about standing firm in Berlin, standing firm in the Far East, standing up to Khrushchev, but he never mentions standing firm in Cuba—and if you can't stand up to Castro, how can you be expected to stand up to Khrushchev?" The crowd went wild.[5]

If anybody had an unassailable anti-red resume, it was Dick Nixon. It's worth noting that Nixon, as a callow congressman from California, served on the House Un-American Activities Committee, the committee that Tail Gunner Joe McCarthy drove to the nadir of cold war paranoia, and ultimately to his own personal ruin. It's also worth remembering that while Fidel was absorbing press hosannas during his first unofficial visit to the States in April of 1959, Nixon came away from a private meeting with the Cuban with an entirely different impression. "Castro is either incredibly naïve about Communism," Nixon wrote, "or is under Communist discipline."[6]

Imagine Nixon's quandary. Imagine Nixon's frustration. His Democratic opponent for the highest office in the land took every chance that presented itself to turn the tables of red-baiting on the old red-baiter himself. Nixon, well into the inner circle of the Cuba Project's planning, was forced to keep his mouth shut, no matter how weak it made him look. In an October foreshadowing of coming events, Kennedy's people put out a statement that suggested the candidate was in favor of unilateral action against the Castro government. Liberals were outraged. Eventually, Kennedy was forced to dial down the rhetoric on Cuba but with only a couple of weeks left before the election, the die had been cast and the candidate's true feelings were a matter of public record.[7]

CIA chief Allen Dulles had been up till then kept deliberately in the dark about the Castro assassination plot and about the agency's active involvement with the mob. When Richard Bissell and Sheffield Edwards briefed the director of central intelligence and his deputy, General Charles P. Cabell, they discussed the plans in terms of (no names, please) A, B, and C, but both Bissell and Edwards left the meeting with the idea that Dulles and Cabell knew exactly what was going down.[8]

The plan gained momentum in the autumn of 1960. After his late summer meeting with Robert Maheu, in October Johnny Rosselli landed in Miami. And since there was no more suitable hostel for the self-respecting hoodlum, he put up at the Hotel Fontainebleau. Rosselli arranged a one-on-one sit-down with Santo Trafficante. Mafioso to Mafioso, Johnny didn't waste words. With his bottomless skills, charm to burn, and killer instinct, Rosselli knew he had the right man in Santo Trafficante.

A short time later, Rosselli introduced Maheu to the two men he had selected to back him up on the Castro hit: Sam Gold and another man who went by the name of Joe. That Joe was Trafficante and Gold turned out to be Sam "Momo" Giancana,[9] also known as "Mo," and also known but only among family and close friends as "Mooney" due to his phosphorescent temper.

Mooney started in the Chicago Outfit taking his orders from Murray "the Camel" Humphreys, Al Capone's political fixer and right-hand man.[10] At the age of twenty, Mooney had probably murdered more men than he could remember. Nasty, short, and brutish, Giancana was a triggerman on the most infamous gangland rubout of all time, the St. Valentine's Day Massacre.[11] By 1960, he had amassed as much power and generated more fear than any racketeer in the country.

Trafficante later claimed that Johnny reached out to him so that he could act as an interpreter. Maybe; Trafficante did speak fluent Spanish.[12] But more usefully, and more believably, Trafficante could function as a middleman between CIA interests and radical Cuban elements in South Florida who were thrilled to do the big job on Fidel. When Rosselli told him about the purpose of the sit-down, Santo thought that whacking Fidel was a swell idea. He felt some patriotic stirrings of his own: "I figure it was like a war."[13]

Santo Trafficante, the bald, bespectacled, crime kingpin in the rumpled suits, designed himself to drift under the radar. He was highly esteemed by the dean of Havana racketeers, Meyer Lansky, which says a lot about him. He had no tabloid nickname. Santo was old school. Santo was true Mafioso.

Like "honor" and "loyalty," two concepts that have gotten a thorough going-over by mob myth makers across the decades, *omerta* was another ideal these men supposedly adhered to. A close translation of the Italian might yield the English equivalent "manliness," but in contemporary American usage the word has come to stand for a self-imposed code of silence among the practitioners of Our Thing *(Cosa Nostra)*. In Mooney's own enlightened definition, *omerta* meant "you keep your eyes and ears open and your fuckin' mouth shut."[14]

Omerta allegedly drew CIA's Edwards and Bissell to the mob in the first place.[15] But Rosselli, during his first meeting with Big Jim O'Connell, practically pissed his pants with excitement. He pulled O'Connell aside and said, "I'm not kidding, I know who you work for."[16]

Thus went the shadowy linkage: Richard Bissell and Sheffield Edwards to Big Jim O'Connell, O'Connell to Maheu, Maheu to Rosselli, Rosselli to Trafficante and Giancana. Through all the layers, there was agreement on one thing: Do whatever it takes to kill Fidel Castro. "Any way, cannon, pills, tanks, airplanes," Trafficante said. "Anything."[17]

Giancana concurred. "We'll take care of Castro," he bragged to his brother, "One way or another." Mooney also succumbed to sentimental feelings for the United States of America. "I think it's my patriotic duty."[18] His main contribution to the festivities was an injection of common sense. O'Connell wanted Castro to be gunned down in Havana, a real, mob street-hit. The reptilian gangster pointed out, when O'Connell suggested that Castro could be rubbed out in a flurry of bullets, that the most likely result for any theoretical assassin would be death,[19] and it was tough to contract suicide missions.

Johnny floated another idea, something cleaner and quieter. "He suggested slipping Castro a Mickey Finn—if the CIA could make a knockout drop both lethal and slow-acting. That would give the guy who did it a chance to get away." Everybody liked it. Big Jim got the agency's tech services on the job, and they eventually killed some monkeys with the concoction they devised.[20]

Unfortunately, Mooney just couldn't resist patting himself on the back. On October 18, Bissell received an FBI memo that must have alarmed him. Intelligence had revealed that Giancana was shooting off his mouth about being in on the Castro hit.[21] The irony had to have been far too delicious to resist. The federal government, which had relentlessly hounded the mighty-mite of a Mafioso, was now reaching out to him to help do their dirty work.

To their enduring surprise, the mobsters' patriotic assignment held no sway with other areas of government. At around the same time Rosselli was scheming with Giancana and the CIA, the FBI tried to squeeze him into informing for them. They showed him a picture of himself as Filippo Sacco in his rustic hometown in Italy. The message they were sending: you're slick, Johnny, but not that slick, and we know all about you. The racketeer was forced to call on his new friends at the agency to make the G-men go away, and they did. It was a matter of national security.[22]

Giancana had girl troubles, too. He was sweet on Judy Campbell, who, according to Jimmy "The Weasel" Frattiano, "was Johnny's girl. Johnny was the one that introduced everybody to everybody." Judy met Frank Sinatra through Rosselli. Sinatra then passed her off to Mooney and Jack Kennedy, who also had an affair with her.[23] It was hard to keep track of these party girls. But Giancana's main squeeze was the singer Phyllis McGuire. Giancana wanted the room of comedian Dan Rowan bugged. In case Phyllis wandered in there one night, Mooney could presumably confront her with recorded, squeaking bedsprings. The CIA agreed to pay for the job, and Maheu handed it off to a private detective. Maheu had his own reasons to be concerned. Sam might have blabbed to Judy. He might have opened up his thin lips to Phyllis, too, in a postcoital chat. Worse still, had Phyllis passed on this irresistible tidbit to her own pals?[24]

So much for keeping "your eyes and ears open and your fuckin' mouth shut."

Sam Giancana wasn't the only security leak that the CIA suffered in the fall of 1960, and the Castro plot wasn't the only prong of the Cuba Project that the agency failed to keep under wraps. The number of men needed for the invasion force kept swelling. Four hundred became six hundred, then seven hundred and fifty, until the figure was over a thousand. Obviously, as the number went up and more people knew about the plan, the secret became harder to keep.[25]

Brigade 2506 recruits were also training just south of Miami at a base in Homestead, pretty much out in the open. When a bunch of kids threw firecrackers over the fence as a gag, they drew gunfire and one teenager was wounded. This boneheaded exchange earned the attention of the *Miami Herald*, especially after the paper learned that the charges against the trigger-happy trainees had been dropped. The *Herald* put a man on the story.[26]

The reporter, David Kraslow, did a bang-up job. He learned that the Homestead camp was only one link in the chain. The Departments of Justice and State were aware of the goings on, too, and they weren't happy about it. Both bureaus were squeezing the Eisenhower administration to shift military efforts out of the country to prevent further violations of the Neutrality Act. And finally, Kraslow's reporting revealed the true nature and purpose of the Homestead base: the men were part of a military invasion force set to ship out and topple the Castro government. Kraslow's editors knew they were onto something hot, but they were troubled by the national security issues that publication of the piece might raise. They reached out to White House officials for direction. None came. Kraslow and his boss finally met with Allen Dulles, who explained that publication of the story would seriously wound national interest. The *Herald* spiked the story.[27]

But at this point, almost the entire Cuban exile community knew what was in the works, and so did the FBI. On the trail of Castro operatives one night, Bill Kelly followed the men to a local bar. Before long, one of the Cubans split off with a pair of American guys. Figuring something was up, he tailed the trio to CIA headquarters in Coral Gables, where the agents complained they had an FBI man on their asses. Kelly was called off.[28]

The agency faced another stumbling block with its black flights in and out of Opa-Locka airport. The runways were darkened, and operatives employed the hub for takeoffs and landings of military-type transport planes. Miami FBI had a pretty clear idea of what was going on. But Kelly and Holloman, concerned with controlling *pro*-Castro agents, would have ceded any action to their Tamale Squad opposites on the *anti*-Castro side. In any event, contact was made between the upper echelons of both agencies. CIA gave the bureau a heads-up: stay out of the way. And Howard Hunt, for one, operated without any FBI interference.[29]

Internal CIA documentation refers to this liaison. In addition to the FBI, the agency kept the Coast Guard and Customs and Immigration in the loop. "Cooperation with all of these officials was excellent," a memo says. "They showed an awareness of the importance of the work and a desire to do what they could to help."[30]

But on the street level, the level that matters, there was no interagency cooperation at all. In Bill Holloman's opinion, the information the Tamale Squad was collecting should have been vetted through the CIA. The G-man got stonewalled at every turn. If he tried to broach the subject with an agency op, the CIA man would plead pig ignorance and lie in Holloman's face. Zero intelligence flowed the other way. "We found out more on Flagler Street than we could learn from CIA," Holloman said. "We could go down to some of our contacts or just friendly people [in Little Havana] and they'd tell you all about the invasion that was coming and where they were training and who was out there and what kind of weapons they had."[31]

So while Allen Dulles may have convinced the *Herald* to do its part for national security and stay mum on the "covert" base, the Cuban exile community was laboring under no such compunctions. Not only had the secret slipped out of the black bag, it was being discussed enthusiastically, and details from Guatemala continued to leak back to Miami.

The Tamale Squad had no end of hassles with agency operatives flying between Havana and Miami. "We kept a pretty tight watch on the [Miami International] airport," Bill Holloman said. "We would get some suspicious guy coming through and we'd pull him aside and take him to the back room down at the end of one of these concourses and he would deny everything." The usual cover was Department of Agriculture or IBM "or some bullshit." And since Holloman knew full well there were "[Cuban] agents going back and forth, if you're CIA,"—he'd inform the spook—"just tell us and you walk out the door and we'll forget you were ever here. And they wouldn't do it."

Holloman would invariably be given a number in Washington to call and the party on the other end would pick up with a deadpan hello, as if the number belonged to some private residence. "Look, we've got this guy down here and if he's CIA or some other official person, just tell us. We don't wanna harass him, but he ain't leaving here till somebody vouches for him." There would be a long wait. Finally, somebody would get back on the line and say, "I can't tell you exactly who he is, but uh, he's official."

Holloman couldn't get over CIA's paranoia. "They just screwed themselves. We were not trying to interfere with them at all. A lot of the time, we really wanted to tell them things." He had let an operative in on the fact that Miami FBI knew of their bases and recruiting offices and suggested that, just maybe, it might be a good idea to move. Holloman was met with stone-faced denial. "It was almost slapstick," he said. "Unfortunately, a lot of good guys got killed."[32]

9

THE ORPHAN
OF FAILURE

he tight presidential race raged into the autumn of 1960. The Cuban issue did not go away. Kennedy pledged his support to "non-Batista democratic anti-Castro forces." He also said that "forces fighting for freedom in exile and in the mountains in Cuba should be sustained and assisted."[1] And although, as has been noted, he was ultimately obliged to soften his language, he refused to take the military option off the table. Kennedy's people had heard the rumors coming out of Miami, too, and they were petrified that if the invasion launched before the election, Nixon would claim all the credit and their man would be sunk.[2]

Kennedy was all about confronting the status quo. He wanted to attack cold war realities head-on. Eisenhower and the Republicans were old stuff, dull, timid. Ike had had his shot, and he blew it. "Action was about to replace inaction," Stephen Ambrose wrote. "Kennedy promised to get the country moving again. Where to, no one knew precisely."[3]

Even after American diplomacy fell down in 1958, officials were committed to a third way of government in Cuba—the way of moderation that excluded extreme elements from both the right and the left. This third way was supposedly represented by the Frente of Artime and his compatriots, and they were heartened by the words that fell from

Kennedy's lips. Frente leader Antonio (Tony) Varona was a tough customer, a former student leader who grew up to be Carlos Prio Socarrás's prime minister. He had, since Castro's first days, lashed out at Fidel for failing to hold elections.[4] He was a proud, passionate man, a bit of a loose cannon, and as a Cuban politician who needed to be managed, the biggest pain in Howard Hunt's ass. But, nearing November 1960, Tony Varona and Manuel Artime were all the way with JFK.[5] Their misplaced enthusiasm would prove to be a bitter irony.

Three days before the U.S. election, a Gallup poll showed the presidential contest to be a statistical dead heat: Kennedy took 50.5 percent and Nixon, 49.5. Kennedy's final number was very close to the Gallup prediction; he did not take 50 percent of the electorate. The winning tally was 49.72 percent on the popular side (a third-party candidate siphoned off half a million ballots) but it was more than Nixon got, and Kennedy's comfortable margin of 303 votes to Nixon's 219 in the electoral college was more than enough to swing the decision his way.[6]

By the time Kennedy was elected, security and any semblance of secrecy regarding the Cuba Project was blown. Awareness of the CIA's supposedly clandestine operation was spreading far wider than the exile community in Miami. The November 19, 1960, issue of the *Nation* ran an editorial under the headline "Are We Training Cuban Guerrillas?" that reported the findings of a Stanford professor, Dr. Ronald Hilton. Hilton said that it was common knowledge in Guatemala that the United States had acquired a huge tract of land in Retahuleu, and the property was being used as a base to train a Cuban counterinsurgency.

The *Nation*, while "pretending no first-hand knowledge of the facts," felt that it was their duty to drag "this dangerous and hair [sic] brained project" out into the light of public scrutiny. The magazine conceded, disingenuously, that the American government might have been unaware of what was taking place in the Guatemalan mountains. If that was the case, the reports "should be checked immediately by all U.S. news media with correspondents in Guatemala."[7]

Aghast at the prospect of Castro's beacon of liberty being scrubbed from the Caribbean, the *Nation* did its best to alert all responsible parties. The magazine was virtually ignored. Armed with the editorial, the only thing the *New York Times* did with the information was run the allegations by the Guatemalan president. Not surprisingly, he denied the charges.[8]

Some historians are quite dismayed that nobody took the *Nation* seriously. Had the wider public been informed, or so this line of thinking goes, Americans would have mobilized in righteous indignation, spurred by the mighty *New York Times* into thwarting this march to military folly. That's a silly idea. Warren Hinckle and William Turner's rich and entertaining work on this period, *The Fish is Red*, is naïve on this matter, almost quaint. The writers presume that the opinions of some Stanford professor were going to affect U.S. policy. With all the wheels in motion, a bunch of sign carriers shouting slogans was supposed to shut down the huge mechanism CIA had assembled in Florida, Guatemala, Honduras, and Nicaragua? Not likely.[9]

What Hinckle and Turner probably didn't know was that the *Times* had already been hoodwinked once, in December 1959, with its "Cuba Invasion Called Imminent" story that quoted *Revolución*. Fidel Castro had been fulminating about a United States invasion since about the second or third week after his takeover. This was the result of his obsession with creating a threat from *without*, something he understood (quite shrewdly) that all successful revolutions need, especially those that are nationalist in nature. Bear in mind that when the first "Morganoso" fell flat, Castro agents recruited the Doughnut Army. And maybe, if not for Tamale Squad regular Bob Dwyer and other federal agents, Castro would have inherited another sixty or so bodies, including Dave "Rum and Sunshine" Hoffman, to place before his firing squads. In the process, Castro would have notched another win in the propaganda column.

The irony is that this time Castro wasn't crying wolf.

In January 1961, president-elect Kennedy received what would have been at least his second briefing by CIA director Allen Dulles on the Cuba Project. A scant two days after he was sworn in, he met again with Dulles and other national security people. The Cuban window was closing. Castro's influence was growing throughout Latin America. But if actual U.S. armed forces invaded the island, Peking and Moscow would be obliged to make other moves in the western hemisphere—though nobody said what exactly these moves might be. And the Cubans training in Guatemala were getting itchy.

JFK well understood that presidents are remembered more for their foreign policy than anything else. He firmly intended to be his own secretary of state. Toward that end, he settled on the nonconfrontational and subordinate Dean Rusk for the (titular) post.[10] Still, within the administration, the conflict over so forward-leaning a move as a Cuba invasion was inevitable. The CIA and Defense Department were convinced the plan was a winner. The State Department fretted.[11] But to anybody who was paying attention during the campaign or to JFK's hatless inaugural address in which he vowed to "pay any price, bear any burden, meet any hardship" and all the rest of it, the coming Cuba invasion was of a piece with the vision he had articulated for at least a year.

While planning and training of troops was being conducted in Miami and Guatemala, CIA was attempting to arm a Cuban underground resistance movement. The agency had purchased and refitted a pair of yachts for the Key West–Havana run that had become so regular one CIA man compared it to a UPS route.[12]

Unfortunately, many of the arms and supplies bound for a force that was assembled in the mountains were intercepted by Castro's men. Other shipments, delivered by prearranged air drop, so badly missed their marks that Cuban peasants fell on them and used them for themselves. And finally, the frenetic freelance activity conducted across the Florida Strait—serious arms runs not connected to agency efforts— was getting picked off by the Coast Guard, or the infiltrators running the missions were killed by Castro forces if they did, in fact, make it to Cuba.

Howard Hunt had no faith in this underground element. "At that point I had no idea how many men, if any, we had dispatched for underground work on the island," he wrote. "But my own survey of Cuba had persuaded me that we could expect little effective help from the general populace."[13]

As the winter of 1961 ground on, Brigade 2506 troops training in Guatemala were close to mutiny. The brigade's fractious character was grounded in the history and nature of Cuban politics: there were those who had joined the army when Prío was in power and had been betrayed by Batista, and there were those who had fought alongside Castro's rebel forces. Some had never served in the military at all and had abandoned civilian careers for the opportunity to fight Castro.[14]

At Base Trax, the rank and file was convinced that maverick Frente member Tony Varona was sowing dissension to consolidate his own power within the group, power he hoped to carry into a post-Castro Cuba. No member of the Frente had been to Trax in months, and that fired suspicions even further. Hunt was dispatched to Guatemala, along with Frente leaders, to squash the brewing revolt.

Varona ripped the brigade's military leadership. Pepe San Roman, their commander and a career officer, had served with Batista's army during the time of the revolution, but he was no Batistano. Artime was originally attracted to him because San Roman was plotting a coup of his own *against* Batista when Castro took over. But Varona hated Batista even more than he hated Castro. It was Batista's second coup that overthrew Carlos Prío Socarrás, under whom Varona had held the prime minister's position. These nasty feelings illustrate why the Frente was such a hornet's nest in the first place; old loyalties and longstanding rivalries set aside for political expedience make for the strangest of bedfellows.

During one meeting, Artime and Varona tore into one another. Artime took a realistic view of the American involvement. He had come to understand, reluctantly maybe, that the CIA was their one and only hope. But Varona, sounding a tired and often-heard note, insisted that the only thing he needed from the Americans was money.[15] Artime argued that the most critical element of the Frente's mission in Guatemala was to show the troops that the politicians had full faith and confidence in the brigade, its officers, and the Americans.[16]

By some estimates, including that of President Igidoras of Guatemala (presidents came and went quickly in Guatemala), the CIA-trained Cuban force was the toughest fighting unit in all of Latin America. But the troops were in danger of overtraining. They had nothing else to do, and risked slipping over that razor's edge of peak combat readiness. No invasion date had been set, increasing tension and leading to speculation among the men that they might never get the chance to fight.

The brigade was ordered into formation one morning, and San Roman addressed them. Then the politicians took their turns. Artime delivered his speech with characteristic passion, praising the soldiers and their American comrades. He promised to join them in combat (and shipped out days later for further training in Mexico).[17]

It was now Varona's opportunity to address the men. In Hunt's mind, "This was the moment that could make or break our plans. But now instead of rebuke and vitriol, Tony heaped praise on the brigade and its leaders, and said the Frente and the exile community were proud of them." He then led the men in the Cuban national anthem. San Roman called attention. The troops straightened. San Roman and Oliva snapped salutes to Artime, Varona, and another Frente member. Hunt's mission, with Varona's cooperation, had been accomplished.[18]

The Kennedy administration continued to push for the inclusion of Manuel Ray in any post-Castro government. Ray had served as Castro's sabotage expert, but having turned against Fidel, as had so many of his former comrades, Ray now represented the "liberal" point of view—at least as far as Kennedy's people were concerned. Hunt remained violently opposed to him, especially after his visit to Base Trax. Ray had zero support among the brigade, and Hunt warned that if Ray's Miami group were folded into the Frente, "it's entirely possible we might find ourselves with a large Miami political organization and no troops at all."[19]

At a March 11 meeting, Dulles apprised Kennedy of the dangers of ditching the Cuba Project. "If we have to take these men out of Guatemala we will have to transport them to the United States, and we can't have them wandering around the country telling everyone what they have been doing." Beyond being a security headache, this presented Kennedy with a political conundrum, too. The Cuban exile community, not just the men training in Guatemala, would be livid if Kennedy called off the operation. And the Republicans would accuse him of faintness of heart. "Anyway," Peter Wyden wrote of the meeting, "the first move was to persuade the exiles to set up a more representative, more liberal political front [and this is where Manuel Ray came in]. The achievement was still eluding Howard Hunt and [Frank Bender]."[20]

Bender, the CIA's other point man, could not find a way to get along with the Frente. The enmity was mutual. The Cuban distaste for Bender sank to hatred as the brigade's anticipated go-date grew near though there was no official word, merely speculation. Agency higher-ups lost patience with Bender, too, and Hunt was himself skating on thin ice.[21]

A CIA op pseudonymously known as Jim Noble was dispatched to Miami to force the Frente to iron out their differences and make itself into a true "government in exile."[22] Noble's solution, probably not of his own making, included Manuel Ray. Hunt and Bender, the old cold warriors, were appalled.

CIA machinations had brought Ray and his group to Florida, much in the way that Artime had been exfiltrated before him. Once in the United States, Ray and his people, known as the MRP, maintained that the Castro revolution had originally been democratic in nature. They would have a tough time making the case for mass executions and class warfare as being in any way "democratic," but still, Ray argued that July 26 had gone wrong under Communist influence. His bleatings fell on sympathetic State Department ears. Administration officials were willing to adopt Ray's viewpoint as their own. In Hunt's opinion, Ray and his people were hard leftists.[23] Their vision of a post-Castro Cuba did not include the reinstatement of the constitution of 1940. Not that anybody read that document after it was written, but still it *did* exist and could have served as a template for Cuban democracy. This lead to the widespread characterization of Ray's movement as *Fidelismo sin Fidel,* or Castroism without Castro.

Ray was wounded by the charges. "I don't know what it means to be a leftist," Ray stated. "If it means to be in favor of all the people and for the welfare of the masses, then I am." Hunt tartly noted that Fidel Castro himself could not have said it better.[24]

At around the same time that Noble was dispatched to Miami, Hunt was ordered to Washington for a sit-down with his CIA superiors. Though they were old friends, covert operations deputy Tracy Barnes applied the pressure, and so did Barnes's boss, Dick Bissell. But Hunt could not (or would not) accept the administration's imposition of Manuel Ray on Frente leadership. He argued that the Americans had already taken everything away from the Cubans. The exiles had submitted to American military planning and political maneuvering. "We've trampled heavily on the pride of men who, in their own country, have been distinguished, highly respected citizens." These men realized, he told Bissell, that they were not much more than "puppets," but they also understood that the CIA was the only hope for their homeland. Hunt could not maintain their evaporating good faith while injecting Manuel Ray into the forefront of exile leadership, in effect, making him an equal. Barnes and Bissell understood. They said they were sorry. Howard Hunt was gone.[25]

Noble had the same difficulty that Hunt and Bender had experienced in moving the Frente past its bickering. In order to get the Cubans on the same page, Noble wrote up what amounted to a two-minute "ultimatum." The document was read by contract operative Wells Cart, a man who spoke perfect Spanish, but the words on the page bore little resemblance to polite Castilian. "If you don't come out of this meeting with a committee, you just forget the whole fuckin' business, because we're through."[26] The power play worked. The Frente was finished, and out of its ashes rose the Cuban Revolutionary Council, or CRC. Kennedy's people got their wish. Manuel Ray was among its leaders.[27]

While the Maheu-Rosselli-Trafficante axis kept at its grim task, Frente member Tony Varona busied himself with extracurricular activities: arming that elusive underground force in Cuba. One Varona-directed gun run was turned back by the Coast Guard, his subgroup's radio transmissions intercepted, but Tony had a scheme. He hoped to use the missions as a bargaining chip. After Brigade 2506 landed and the exile politicians were established as a government in arms, Varona could crow about his valuable contribution and thrust himself into post-Castro primacy.[28]

Toward the middle of March, the boxers Floyd Patterson and Ingemar Johannson were slugging it out for the heavyweight championship. Their third bout was held in Miami Beach, and Rosselli, Giancana, and Maheu were in town for the fight. Santo Trafficante paid a call to their Fontainebleau suite, and he had a distinguished guest in tow. Guess who came to dinner? Tony Varona.[29]

Our story so far: Big Jim O'Connell had gotten the pills and the money to Maheu. Maheu delivered the poison to Rosselli. Rosselli was supposed to get the stuff to Trafficante, and Varona, as Santo's bagman, would make sure that yet another shady Cuban exile, a man named Macho Grener, took it from there. Maheu saved the grandest gesture for himself. In the hotel room, he unlatched a briefcase and dumped ten grand in Tony's lap.[30]

Varona's man Macho Grener had recruited a cook in one of Fidel's favorite restaurants. The poison must somehow have made it into the kitchen man's hands, or at least that's what Maheu thought. Things looked good for a hot minute. Press reports of a Castro illness led Maheu to believe his team had connected, and he called an associate to chirp about their victory. But Fidel made a miraculous recovery and then stopped eating at the restaurant where Grener's hit man was in place, maybe because the cooking made him sick.[31] Food poisoning, indeed. Grener's man might have lost his nerve, and Fidel's malady might have been a coincidence, but the Castro hit was supposed to coordinate with the landing of Brigade 2506. It's also possible that Grener's Havana contact was waiting for word of a go-date that never came, and that the indecision cost the CIA and its mob hit-team their best whack at Castro.[32] Happily, it would hardly be their last.

Howard Hunt might have been advocating Castro's elimination from day one, but he knew nothing about the plot to kill him, was in the dark about Varona's ties to the mob, and hit the ceiling when he found out about the Cuban's gun-running. Tony's wildcat operations were not CIA-sanctioned and brought heat on the other arms-transfer missions, which were not really accomplishing anything, anyway. Tony Varona's double-dealing was all about one man, Tony Varona, and by this stage in the Cuba Project, the left hand didn't know what the right hand was doing. CIA might have fumbled security in the wider world, but they were great at keeping secrets from themselves.

A s the winter of 1961 turned to spring, John F. Kennedy vacillated. Weighing the best advice he could get, Kennedy wanted to reserve the right to call off the whole thing even twenty-four hours prior to the launch. He could not or would not guarantee the leaders of Brigade 2506 overt military support. They wanted to go ahead anyway.[33]

Senator J. William Fulbright of Arkansas had JFK's ear from when they had served together on the Senate Foreign Relations Committee. In March, Fulbright, who had heard the rumblings of a coming Cuban invasion, wrote an almost four-thousand-word memo decrying the plan. The senator thought it was an atrocious idea.[34]

Chester Bowles, a State Department dove and Dean Rusk's number two, remained stridently opposed to any Cuban invasion. In a March 31 memo to Secretary Rusk, Bowles wrote, "A great deal of time and money has been spent and many individuals have become emotionally involved in its success. We should not, however, proceed with this adventure simply because we are wound up and cannot stop."[35]

On Tuesday, April 4, a meeting was held in a small room at State Department headquarters in Foggy Bottom. Kennedy, still uncertain about the wisdom of an invasion, convened a sounding board. Dick Bissell briefed the president on the brigade's combat readiness. Everybody else listened. When he was done talking, the questions came in rapid fire. Kennedy went around the room and asked each man his opinion. Dean Rusk seemed for it. Fulbright was aghast. Adolf Berle, a Latin American specialist who dated back to the Roosevelt administration, said, "I say, let 'er rip."[36]

The trial of Francisco "The Hook" Molina started on March 7, 1961, with Alexander Hermann prosecuting for the State of New York. Samuel Newburger represented Molina. The Honorable Mitchell Schweitzer presided, and the charge was murder in the first degree.

In his opening statement, Hermann said that Molina started the fight that led to Magdalena Urdaneta's death with the hysterical threat that nobody would leave El Prado alive. Newburger insisted that an anti-Castro woman touched off the brawl by insulting the July 26ers. When the counselor cross-examined the prosecution's witnesses about their political activities, many were obliged to fall back on their Fifth Amendment rights against self-incrimination. The jury heard many accounts of the incident from people who were at El Prado on the afternoon in question; several testified that they had seen Molina with a gun.[37]

"One of the witnesses," Bill Kelly remembered, "was a nineteen-year-old Cuban boy from Miami, who was in the restaurant when the murder took place." Hermann gauged the kid essential to his case. But Hermann had a problem. "It so happens that this nineteen-year-old boy is with the brigade down in Guatemala. So [the prosecutor's office] contacted [the FBI] and the State Department and the CIA," Kelly said. The agency's response was predictable. "You can't have him. He could compromise this plan that we've got, and we're not going to let him go."

In the end, Alexander Hermann prevailed. The kid was flown from Guatemala to Miami, and Kelly was assigned to make sure he got to New York. He headed to Opa-Locka airport in the dead of night, turned down a nearby dirt road, and drove an eighth of a mile. He stopped as per prearranged instructions, killed his headlights, and waited for contact. It came in the form of two shotguns, one on either side of the car, pointed at Kelly's head.

The FBI man showed the agents his credentials. They ordered him to stay where he was. A panel truck backed up. "They unlock the door," Kelly said, "and out comes this nineteen-year-old kid in battle fatigues. He hadn't even changed his clothes. They say, 'Okay, Kelly, he's yours. And if anything happens, it's your ass.'"

Kelly drove the young Cuban into Miami, where his parents lived, and took the calculated risk of leaving him there unguarded. He went home and went to bed. "I'm praying that this guy doesn't do anything stupid overnight," and he didn't. Kelly drove back the next morning and physically placed the Cuban on a nonstop flight to New York, where agents from the New York field office escorted him to court.[38] Brigade 2506 left Guatemala without him. It may well have saved his life.

Molina's trial lasted a month. Then, at three o'clock on the afternoon of April 6, the jury sent a note to Judge Schweitzer. They were uncertain on how to distinguish the difference between first- and second-degree murder. The question was a dark omen for the defense. Shortly before midnight, the jurors filed back to their box. Schweitzer asked them if they had reached a verdict. They replied that they had. Guilty of murder in the second degree.[39]

Five days later, as Brigade 2506 was being transported from Guatemala to Nicaragua, their final launch point, President Kennedy held a press conference. The first words out of a reporter's mouth had to do with United States military action against Cuba, which, of course, Kennedy denied. But he left himself some room to squirm. He said that there would be no combat operations by the United States military, which was true. Technically. The CIA's operational planners were encouraged. They were positive that tough-guy Kennedy, when confronted with the facts of a battlefield, would send in the Marines before he allowed the brigade to be defeated on the beachhead.[40]

10

WHAT MIGHT HAVE STOOD HAD I NOT FALLEN

he brigade's troopships left Puerto Cabezas, Nicaragua, and sailed across the Caribbean on April 13, 1961. Their plans had already been altered. The idea of a Cuban domestic force, an underground linking up with invading exiles, had by this time been abandoned. There would be no internal support on the beachhead because, according to some, there was no underground to speak of. This force, Howard Hunt said in an interview, was little more than "a figment of the imagination."[1]

Original CIA estimates put Castro in command of about fifteen World War II vintage B-26 bombers, a half dozen "ancient" Sea Furies, and three Lockheed T-33 fighter jets. Aerial surveillance photos taken on April 14 revealed Castro's unimpressive air force, the Fuerza Aerea Revolucionaria, or FAR, idling at three separate bases. The planes were compared to ducks on a pond, and at dawn the next day, April 15, they were attacked by the brigade's B-26s.[2]

The Cuban exiles' reaction was delirious. Finally, *finally*, something was happening. Men in Miami couldn't get to recruitment offices fast enough. Everybody wanted a piece of the action.[3] Later that morning, the agency crash-landed one plane near Key West and brought back another, all shot up, to Miami. According to CIA disinformation, these planes were piloted by Cuban defectors and had strafed Castro's airfields before turning north toward Florida and asylum. This fairy tale was, of course, cover for the actual bombing that *CIA-trained* Cubans had carried out against FAR planes. Reporters were allowed to view the one aircraft on a Miami runway, but a few sharp-eyed scribes noticed the difference between what was supposed to be an FAR plane and the ones they knew the agency was flying. (The CIA planes had metal noses, the FAR aircraft, plastic ones; it was also clear that the B-26's guns hadn't been fired.) The story didn't go over with those present, but the Associated Press put out a dispatch corroborating this Byzantine deception.[4]

Miami News reporter and CIA "asset" Hal Hendrix weighed in with his own chunk of disinformation. "It has clearly been established now," the old cold warrior wrote on April 15, "that there will be no mass invasion against Cuba by the anti-Castro forces gathered at bases in Central America and this country. The *News* has stated this for several months."[5]

Total air superiority for Brigade 2506 was presumed from the very first stages of military planning. There was always supposed to be at least one other set of sorties by brigade planes, to soften up the beachhead at Playa Giron, the ultimate landing point for ground troops. But Kennedy gave word that the approval of any further action had to go through the office of the secretary of state. On Saturday night, April 16, General Charles Cabell and Richard Bissell went to Dean Rusk's office. Rusk, deeply conflicted over the Cuba Project from the second he had heard about it, told them that he had just gotten off the phone with the president. Rusk told Kennedy he opposed the second set of strikes. Kennedy concurred.[6]

The Cuban air force had not been destroyed. Far from it. FAR's most lethal components, those T-33 jets, sat gleaming and unscathed at a base near Santiago.[7] On Sunday afternoon, April 17, at CIA headquarters in Washington, reality—and trouble—intruded. The newest aerial surveillance photos of Castro's air force were being reviewed, and it was obvious "from the tense atmosphere," Hunt wrote, "that the [agency's] Cuban pilots had claimed more destruction than had actually occurred."[8]

With Allen Dulles out of the country (plausible deniability again), his deputy director, Charles Cabell, fresh from a round of golf—and, with Dulles gone, in charge at CIA—had dropped by headquarters to see how the invasion was proceeding. "This chance decision"—Cabell's informal visit—Hunt said, "was to affect the destinies of men and nations from that point on."[9] CIA planners begged Cabell to order another bombing mission. Cabell countered that he had no authorization to do so, but then capitulated, going all the way up the chain of command that stopped with Kennedy. But JFK was already wilting in the heat of the political fallout from Peking and Moscow over Friday morning's attack. He issued a flat no.[10] "The first chill of awareness," Hunt wrote, "that disaster had suddenly become possible now gripped us all."[11]

That second air strike—the one that never came—on the morning of April 17, 1961, spelled disaster for Brigade 2506, and the CIA men knew it. "Failure to make air strikes in the immediate beachhead area the first thing in the morning (D-Day)," they advised, "would clearly be disastrous."[12] Most likely, it would mean their invasion was doomed. They were right about that.

The brigade's CIA liaison, Gray Lynch, was bothered by what he was looking at through his binoculars. Aboard the ship *Blagar,* instead of a darkened beach, Lynch was peering at an arc-lit strip of sand that looked to him "like Coney Island." Nearby stood a thicket of trees that might be camouflaging any kind of ambush. This warranted further investigation. Lynch and a small crew piloted an inflatable landing craft toward the beach, and as they drew nearer, a jeep appeared on the sand. Instead of driving past, the vehicle stopped, beamed its headlights toward the sea, and froze the brigade's frogmen in their glow. Lynch and his team poured fire into the vehicle, killing two of Castro's local militiamen. The first shots at the Bay of Pigs, in spite of all Kennedy's apprehensions, had been fired by an American.[13]

Back aboard the *Blagar* after his raid, Lynch received a message from CIA headquarters. "Castro still has operational aircraft," the communication stated. Unload all ships and supplies and take ships to sea as soon as possible." Lynch wasn't worried.[14] He knew United States air power was vastly superior to Castro's juryrigged FAR, and anyway, he expected the airfields to be destroyed. It was, after all, in the plan.

CIA remained distrustful of Manuel Ray, now a member of the recently formed CRC. The agency was still unconvinced that Ray was loyal to *la causa*; they couldn't swear Ray wasn't going to report back to Castro, especially after the council began "clamoring," in Hunt's word, for advance information on the invasion. Hunt suggested the CRC be sequestered until the beachhead was secured and the provisional government recognized by the United States. His plan was approved.

Frank Bender had assembled Manuel Ray, Tony Varona, and provisional president Dr. Jose Miro Cardona, among other CRC members, in New York. He told them they were going to be put on ice until after the invasion, and that if anybody wanted to leave, now was their chance. They all stayed. They were then flown to Opa-Locka and kept under guard, though the men had no idea where they were and what, exactly, was commencing at Playa Giron.[15]

Brigade 2506 hit the beach at 1:15 A.M. on April 17 behind their commanding officer, Pepe San Roman. His landing was immediately discovered by local militia, and the two sides exchanged gunfire. The one advantage that might have justified the danger of an amphibious landing at night, the element of surprise, was blown. This was the invasion that Fidel Castro had been hysterical about for the last two and a half years. The alarm went out island-wide.[16] And by 6:30 A.M., brigade troops were landing under heavy fire. They were easy targets for the "operational aircraft" Gray Lynch had been warned about five hours earlier. Their launch craft—the ones that weren't crippled by engine failure—were getting hung up on the coral reef near the beach, coral that had been dismissed as "seaweed" during the planning stage. Troopers were forced to carry ammunition and arms, including 640-pound mortars, on their shoulders as they waded the rest of the way ashore.[17]

The *Houston*, which had been hit in an FAR attack, had off-loaded the brigade's Second Battalion, but the inexperienced Fifth Battalion, the last men trained, panicked. Some jumped overboard and drowned, others were attacked by sharks. Still others seemed frozen, unable to disembark the wounded ship. CIA frogman "Rip" Robertson, who had reached the *Houston* in a rubber raft screamed, "Get off you bastards. It's your fucking war."[18]

Castro's Sea Furies, allegedly destroyed, were now in action. The already disabled *Houston* was pounded again. She ran aground. Rocket strikes hit the *Rio Escondido* dead center, and she exploded and sank, taking 145 tons of arms and three thousand gallons of airplane fuel with her to the bottom of the Bay of Pigs.[19] In an interview forty-some years later, Howard Hunt said, "Our battle was lost right there."

In the afternoon, a column of Castro's troops, the 339 Battalion, totaling between seven hundred and nine hundred men, was observed on a highway advancing toward brigade positions. Now came the first contact that San Roman's troops made that day with their limited—and politically hamstrung—air cover, but it proved devastating. Brigade B-26s blew the life out of the 339. Literally. The survivors could not be counted on two hands. The highway was a curtain of fire; the bodies lined the roadside in heaps. "This, indeed," Haynes Johnson noted dryly, "was air support."[20] Or to quote Rip Robertson in another context, *This* is your fucking war.

Moments later, the brigade bomber had a Castro T-33 on his ass. The pilot screamed over his radio for an escort plane to shoot him, but the captain of the other plane replied that he was out of ammo. Both were hit by enemy fire and ditched into the bay. Neither pilot was heard from again.[21]

After the FAR knocked out the *Houston* and sank the *Rio Escondido,* the accompanying brigade ships were ordered out of the area to regroup. By nightfall, San Roman was expecting a resupply effort. He was nearly out of ammunition after a single day of fighting. Blinker signals beamed from the beach brought no response. The commander took a small launch and a radio operator six miles out, screaming at the darkened sea for boats that were not there.[22]

Meanwhile, back in Opa-Locka, the situation at the CRC safe house had grown equally desperate. Bender was hollering down the phone at Hunt, and then at Bissell. One council member threatened suicide unless he was released. Bissell snuffed the fire by securing the White House's permission to dispatch Kennedy officials Adolf "Let 'er Rip" Berle and Arthur Schlesinger to visit the exile leaders in Opa-Locka.[23]

By 4 A.M. Tuesday, April 19, Brigade 2506 was under heavy attack by Castro artillery. This alone might have wiped them out, but San Roman and his second in command, Erneido Oliva, occupied a long narrow position. Dozens of Castro shells overshot their line and landed in the sea. But the enemy kept coming. Hopelessly overmatched at this point, the brigade fought like demons. Oliva opened up with mortar fire, then replaced his rounds with grenades of *fosforo blanco,* white phosphorous, or in army slang "Willie P." This brutal substance is essentially powdered fire that ignites on contact with the air. "The shouting of the enemy at that moment," Oliva said, "was just like hell."[24]

Oliva's troopers came out ahead in that skirmish, but by midmorning the brigade's situation was dire. They were being attacked by massive numbers and were virtually out of ammunition. San Roman received contact from aboard the *Blagar.* He said, "Where the hell have you been, you son of a bitch?"

Gray Lynch came back at him. "We will never abandon you. We will go in and evacuate you."

In the face of overwhelming odds, San Roman remained defiant. "I will not be evacuated," he said. "We will fight to the end here if we have to."[25]

On the evening of the day before, April 18, while the brigade was getting absolutely pounded, Kennedy had showed up at the White House in white tie and tails, having come from a formal dinner. Dick Bissell pushed him for the use of navy ships and navy planes in a desperate attempt to salvage the operation. Kennedy turned him down and later bragged, "They couldn't believe that a new President like me wouldn't panic and try to save his own face. Well, they had me figured all wrong."[26] Tough guy Kennedy prevailed over the experts; his empty victory cost his country decades of hard-won credibility that some would argue it has still not regained, and Vietnam, Iran-Contra, and September 11 were yet to be.

Kennedy was left deeply embittered by the defeat, though his public comments were "philosophical." He broke off a sentence midstream during that midnight meeting, and, wearing his tails, went out to the Rose Garden and brooded. Pierre Salinger, his press secretary, discovered him in his bedroom the next morning in tears. For weeks afterward, the president complained of sleepless nights, "thinking about those poor guys down in Cuba."[27]

Over the decades, the keepers of the Kennedy flame have crowed about his brave decision to accept responsibility for the defeat at Playa Giron. As a White House statement put it, "President Kennedy has stated from the beginning that as President he bears sole responsibility."[28] It was the only decent thing to do. In spite of the lapses in intelligence and errors in execution, the debacle at the Bay of Pigs was, and has been, John F. Kennedy's cross to bear.

At 5 A.M. on Tuesday, April 19, Pepe San Roman and Gray Lunch resumed radio contact, San Roman with his back to the ocean and Lynch still aboard the *Blagar*. "Do you people realize how desperate the situation is? Do you back us or quit?" At 6:42 he said, "C-54 [plane] dropped supplies. All went into the sea. Send more." 9:14 A.M.: "Where the hell is jet cover?" Half an hour later: "Can you throw something into this vital point in the battle? Anything."

The brigade was being cut to pieces by Castro artillery and air power. Pepe's transmissions, though more urgent and despondent with the passage of the day, remained calm. He was a professional military commander to the end. At 2:32 P.M., before the batteries on his portable communications unit died, San Roman sent a last desperate message: "Am destroying all equipment and communications. I have nothing left to fight with. Am taking to the swamps."[30]

A s San Roman was radioing his final dispatches to the *Blagar*, Kennedy administration point men Berle and Schlesinger were landing at Opa-Locka. They were met by Jim Noble and Frank Bender, and taken to meet with the council. Noble thought they were "a pitiful sight." One leader wept as he and Noble embraced. The Cubans were desperate for news from Playa Giron, where they all had brothers, or sons, or cousins involved in the fighting. One begged to be sent to Giron so that he could die on the beaches with his men, but there was no point. The war was over, and they had lost. Varona was white with rage. He announced that he was leaving at noon for Miami to call a press conference, where he would tell the world of this savage betrayal. "Let them shoot me down," Varona said, "if they dare."[31]

Kennedy's "best and brightest" approached the inevitability of the brigade deaths and imprisonment as if it was a public relations conundrum, a fact that was painfully apparent to one council member. "The shit face they sent me," he said, "was only worried about the political popularity of their man."

"The problem that April morning for Schlesinger and Berle," Joan Didion observed in her book *Miami*, "was one of presentation, of damage control. Which is another way of saying that they were worried about the political popularity of their man."[32]

In the end, it was decided to fly the exile leaders to Washington for a White House meeting with Kennedy. Bissell asked Howard Hunt if he would escort them to the sit-down, but Hunt, depressed and sickened by his role in this dirty double-deal, could not face them. Frank Bender drew the miserable assignment instead.[33]

Under the whup-whup-whup of helicopter blades and incessant bursts of machine gun fire, routed brigade forces took refuge in the wooded areas. A lucky few found fresh water in hollowed-out tree stumps or ponds. The less fortunate, and this was the great majority, were reduced to drinking their own urine, or, when they could catch and kill the reptiles, lizard blood. They dined on raw snakes. Castro's army was determined not to go into the woods to flush out the invaders. Starvation and near madness drove them out.[34]

Erneido Oliva was captured on April 23, having endured four days without food or water. Two days after he was taken prisoner, Che Guevara turned up to interrogate him. Guevara wanted to know if Oliva was aware of the penalty for treason, and Oliva said yes: The firing squad. Che pressed. Wasn't Oliva afraid of dying? Oliva said, "Of course I am. I was also afraid of the dentist when he took out four teeth."[35]

Pepe San Roman and Manuel Artime took a number of soldiers into hiding with them, but the men had split into two groups of ten, then four groups of five, until Pepe was alone with just one other man. They had been subsisting on water found under rocks and had even managed, at one point, to kill a cow. They ate the animal's meat until it went rotten in the heat. San Roman ran into a Castro patrol as the local militiamen were wandering around, lost in the woods, on April 25. San Roman surrendered. There was no point left in shooting.[36]

One Castro commander loaded 149 prisoners into a truck and bolted the doors. It was one o'clock in the afternoon on a steaming Cuban day. Nine of the men suffocated on the eight-hour ride to Havana. A tenth died after reaching the destination, and the others survived by punching air vents in the truck's walls with their belt buckles. Castro's man had reasoned that those who didn't survive the ride would be that many more that wouldn't have to be shot.[37]

The U.S. Navy destroyer *Eaton* had been patrolling the Caribbean all that week. Captain Pete Searcy's ship could have been deployed at any time, but only in the aftermath of Giron set off on its mission: search and rescue. The *Eaton* picked up twenty-six survivors along the Cuban coast. The last order Searcy received was to burn the ship's navigation log, the engineering log, and the rest of his mission's documentation, personally. Captain Searcy took them all to the ship's engineering room. He fed them into the incinerator.[38]

On April 23, fifty rescued troopers from Brigade 2506 were flown back to Miami. They landed at Opa-Locka airport, where they exchanged their fatigues for sport shirts. The men were then transported to a house in South Miami by a yellow school bus. Their loved ones picked them up and drove them home. One of the men was summoned to a Frente safe house in Coconut Grove. He was handed an envelope containing three hundred dollars cash and a short time later received an unmarked letter telling him that that was the end of the money.[39]

Kennedy helped hand Fidel Castro a military victory, but the points the Cuban racked up in terms of propaganda could not have been more valuable. He went on television for nearly a week; his "Victory Sunday" television appearance dragged on for four hours as he produced documentation and illustrated his version of the battle with maps and a pointer. A week later, Castro had the captured brigade survivors assembled in the National Sports Palace. The event was, likewise, televised. There he harangued and argued with and humiliated the defeated force, but to his credit, he did not have them all executed (five actually were).[40] He realized that keeping the men alive served two purposes. In the first place, a massacre on this scale would have painted Castro as a butcher and exposed the "purity" of his revolution as a sham. Instead, he received hosannas as a humanitarian. Second, and probably more important, Brigade 2506 was worth money. Lots of it.

Francisco Molina was sentenced to twenty years to life in prison on June 29, 1961. At the same time, negotiations were being conducted between Havana and Washington; Castro had originally demanded $62 million for the release of the prisoners of Brigade 2506. At one point, they were going to be exchanged for American-built tractors, but a deal with the manufacturer could not be reached.[41] And Molina had another short distance to travel before his arc was complete. At sentencing, his lawyer asked that The Hook be repatriated to Cuba in exchange for a valuable prisoner that Castro was unwilling to let go of: Manuel Artime. Judge Schweitzer was outraged. "Under no circumstances," he said, "will this court be a trading post for human beings."[42]

Molina began to serve his sentence in the notorious Sing Sing state prison and was last reported to have been moved farther upstate to Attica. It is exactly there that his trail goes cold. Neither institution has any record of his ever having been there. But an internal CIA memorandum reveals that the federal government and the Cuban cause trumped Judge Schweitzer's protestations. A Castro agent who had been under diplomatic cover at the UN slipped quietly out of the country with Molina and his friend (previously Bill Kelly's bete noire) Jorge Antonio Rodriguez Orihuela "and upon arrival in Cuba tried to obtain employment for both individuals."[43]

Castro's original demand was negotiated down to $53 million worth of food and medicine. The proceedings took the better part of two years. Finally, at about 6 P.M. on Sunday, December 23, 1962, the first military transport plane landed at Homestead Air Force Base. Aboard were the first ransomed veterans of Brigade 2506.[44]

On Saturday, December 29, the brigade, in military formation, assembled at the Orange Bowl. There were forty thousand people in the stands. Many wept. Erneido Oliva presented President Kennedy the flag of Brigada De Assalto 2506. Kennedy, not quite overcome with emotion, vowed that the next time the flag was run up a pole, it would fly over a free Havana.[45] It was probably the right thing to say at the time.

Epilogue

THE LIONS
IN WINTER

he defeat of Brigade 2506 at Playa Giron has long since entered the realm of mythology, of legend, consigned to the mists of fading memory, which is another way of saying it belongs to the romantic heart. The solemn occasion is marked every year by a dwindling number of veterans and their families at 12:01 A.M. on April 17. The names of the fallen and the more recently deceased are read. The faithful and the merely curious then adjourn to the SW 9th Street (Miami) location of the Museum and Library of Brigade 2506. Visiting dignitaries, the few who have any idea of what is being commemorated, offer words of patriotic encouragement to the two or three dozen assembled there.

In 2004, Maryland lieutenant governor Michael Steele addressed a restless group of people that numbered no more than fifty. What, exactly, he was doing at the commemoration, and if any people in the audience had ever heard of him before, remains unclear. The lieutenant governor was terribly late. He apologized, but the man was polished and said the things he thought ought to be said. He received a plaque rewarding him for his service, then, being a man with an extremely tight schedule, shoved off for his next event, protected by two serious-looking Maryland state troopers.

The Maryland attorney Roberto Allen also had the opportunity to speak. His topic, understandably, was the heroic sacrifice made by the martyrs of Brigade 2506, and he spoke of what might have stood had they not fallen. He mocked Castro and Castro's Cuba for the failed Stalinist state that it indisputably and irrevocably has devolved into over the course of his long, dark reign. As of this writing, Castro's control of Cuba is approaching forty-seven years. Forty-seven years. But the bright young lawyer was under the obligation to complete his remarks on a note of hope. He did not falter. "What the United States government and the CIA failed to do" Allen said, "and what the Brigade was prevented from achieving, God himself will one day accomplish."

Wait for it, Habakkuk wrote. It will not be late. It will surely come.

Considering the mournful 1985 iteration of this gathering for her book, *Miami,* Joan Didion compared the participants to "communicants." She could find no idiom beyond religious fervor to convey the zeal of those who had believed— mistakenly it turned out—that John F. Kennedy was a devout congregant in their one true faith. Theirs, she wrote, was a secular communion. The body and blood of patriotism, machismo, and the struggle represented a secular trinity.[1] God will confound the intellectuals. But even a confounded Didion must have understood that what she was reporting on was romance, and romance survives in the heart, and not in the mind.

In a way, it's hard not to be overwhelmed by the Catholicism of it all. This isn't the conclusion of one cockeyed Catholic. Didion certainly picked up on it, and so have other writers. The elements dovetail, from the resolute sanctity of Queen Isabel of Spain, to the staunch religious devotion of Kelly and so many of his colleagues, the Jesuit educations of Artime and Castro, the recitation of the rosary by Erneido Oliva and the brigade troops at Base Trax. The fight against Communism, with Fidel Castro in the foreground, can be read through a squint as a struggle with sin and redemption, of a salvation that has yet to be realized. True Catholicism encompasses many virtues (and failings), of course, but it is, on a very large scale, about romanticism of the most sublime sort.

Bill Kelly was reassigned from the Tamale Squad in September 1962. A few years earlier, J. Edgar Hoover had instituted his Top Jewel Thief Program, and Kelly went to work on major robberies, along with his FBI colleague Bill Holloman, who was his supervisor. On November 1, 1964, G-men kicked in the door of a Brickell Avenue luxury apartment and busted the notorious thief and press darling Jack Rolland Murphy, a.k.a. Murph the Surf. Kelly was posted on a balcony below, the hammer on his service revolver cocked in case the acrobatic Murphy attempted an outdoor escape. He never got that far. J. Edgar was well pleased.

Kelly continued on in his criminal work, making the occasional arrest on violations of the Mann Act, or the interstate transportation of a female for the purposes of prostitution. In June 1972 he was summoned to Washington, D.C. He was one of the initial investigators of the break-in at the Watergate Hotel. The report on his findings took him nine days to write and covered some 250 pages, the first scribbling of an infinite paper trail that would eventually end the presidency of Richard Nixon. Kelly then devoted himself full time to the investigation of obscenity cases, including the signal "porno chic" picture *Deep Throat*. He retired from the bureau in 1980, and since 1981, he has served the Broward County Sheriff's Office as a consultant on the prosecution of obscenity and child pornography. He remains active in this role today as a volunteer.

Besides Bill Kelly, the only survivors of the original Tamale Squad are Bill Holloman and Charles "Tony" Edmiston, but the Miami FBI office still maintains an internal security team devoted to Cuban affairs.[2] The Tamale Squad lives!

Howard Hunt's name will live forever in connection with the aforementioned Watergate burglary, for which he served some three and a half years in federal prison. Among those arrested for the crime were his old friend Bernie Barker and others who have since gone on to infamy in the "Cuban Exile Community." Hunt remains an irresistible target for left- and right-wing nuts of every stripe, conspiracy theorists, and Internet lunatics who have long strived to link him to the assassination of John F. Kennedy.

Hunt hasn't done himself any favors over the years by diabolically suggesting that it didn't matter who pulled the trigger, the important thing was that the job got done. In 1978, *Spotlight* magazine published an article that put Hunt in Dallas on November 22, 1963. Hunt demanded a retraction. The magazine refused. Hunt sued and won a $650,000 judgment, but the case was overturned on appeal, and Hunt was ordered to pay the court costs. The allegations refused to die, and in a 2003 interview, an exasperated and bemused Hunt told me, "Okay, I shot JFK. Now prove it." That way, of course, lies madness.

Howard devoted his later years to writing and has published some two dozen books, many of them pulpy thrillers featuring a romanticized stand-in for E. Howard. He has lately consented to interviews that he holds from his Florida home, where his wife plays hostess to curiosity seekers and Hollywood big shots. His beautiful and charming now-adult children from this second marriage are unfailingly polite. Their love for their aged father is palpable. The Brown graduate, OSS veteran, and vilified CIA fall guy, this lion in winter, has not finished up badly at all.

By the mid-1970s, Meyer Lansky was collecting social security checks and playing gin rummy with his cronies in Miami Beach. He had been deftly portrayed as Hyman Roth in *The Godfather, Part II* by the actor Lee Strasberg. Lansky blew a huge hole in his own myth in 1978 when he said to the *Miami News*, "I can tell you one thing. When I die, they aren't going to find any millions."[3] He wasn't lying. Meyer Lansky left this world in the first days of 1983. His financial legacy, such as it was, was tangled up in his brother Jake's will, and Meyer left his heirs very little. In an irony he would have savored, he beat the long odds of the business he had chosen, and died, as an old man, of natural causes.

Johnny Rosselli's gaseous, murdered remains bobbed to the surface of Biscayne Bay in a barrel in 1975. Mooney Giancana was shot in the back of the head while stirring sausages around a frying pan in his suburban Chicago basement that same year. Santo Trafficante went out quietly in 1986, an old man awaiting heart surgery in a Houston hospital. Bob Maheu is still alive in Las Vegas, Nevada.

Errol Flynn's wicked, wicked ways undid him in 1959. He dropped dead of heart failure, much diminished, at the age of fifty. George Raft fared a bit better. He finished his days in relative obscurity, appearing as an actor in long-forgotten European films, before succumbing to leukemia at the age of eighty-five.

Ernesto "Che" Guevara carried the mantle of armed revolution into the mid-1960s. He somewhat resembled a dog without a home in 1966, marooned in Prague, Czechoslovakia, while emissaries sniffed the Latin American air for the country where Che's brand of leadership would be most useful. Some controversy remains over who made the ultimate decision to go there, but Guevara ended up in Bolivia with a small band of guerrillas. A mix of Bolivians and Cubans, this was a highly undisciplined unit, discovered early on by Bolivian government troops, kept under surveillance, harassed, cut off with no support from Fidel, from the peasantry, or from Bolivian Communists. Guevara, increasingly inhabiting some personal dream world, wrote in April 1967 that "everything resolved itself in the normal matter. Morale is good."[4]

In late September, Guevara led his men straight into an ambush by the Bolivian army. They managed to escape that skirmish, but the end of Che Guevara was inevitable and near. He was taken prisoner on October 8, 1967. He was interrogated, as much as he would allow it, by a Bolivian colonel and by Brigade 2506 veteran and CIA operative Felix Rodriguez. CIA had wanted to keep Guevara alive, but was overridden by the Bolivian army.[5] The order was to execute him. When Rodriguez came to ask Che for his final wishes, his arch nemesis reported that Guevara was prepared to die like a man, and he did, on October 9, 1967.[6]

And so commenced the unkillable myth of Che Guevara. Graffiti appearing around college campuses in the late 1960s proclaimed *Che Viva!* But of course, Che does not *viva;* Che is doornail dead and rests, uneasily perhaps, in an anonymous grave somewhere in Bolivia. His image certainly lives, however, through silkscreen wall hangings, tee-shirts now manufactured in toddler sizes, and in parodies, from *Planet of the Apes* to O'Che, an Irish shamrock replacing the star on his beret. The same broad forehead, the same handsome features, the same black eyes blaze toward the horizon, a legend, a hero, a misguided martyr, a blundering victim of his own wild romantic heart.

The most hated man in Miami remains Fidel Castro, but he is followed closely by John F. Kennedy. Kennedy might not have been half the man, or the president, that his hagiographers would like the world to think he was; neither was he the evil traitor who turned his back on the Cuban cause. He dropped the ball at Playa Giron, yes. But very recently, Erneido Oliva has detailed a proposed sequence of events that would have included the folding of Brigade 2506 into the American armed forces proper. This was but one piece of the Kennedy brothers' Operation Mongoose, a second covert effort to overthrow Fidel Castro. The plan was, from the first, going to include direct U.S. military involvement, but then Kennedy was assassinated. Lyndon Johnson abandoned the plan in 1964.[7]

It is impossible not to feel the romantic pull of the young Fidel Castro's charisma and idealism of the late 1950s. It is equally impossible to defend, in the present tense, his moribund Stalinist regime. The history of Cuban-American relations since the Bay of Pigs is far beyond the scope of this book, but Castro and Castro's Cuba continue to preoccupy Americans. *This day,* June 14, 2005: the lead story in today's *New York Sun* reports on how the European Union has decided not to restore diplomatic sanctions on the Castro government, opting instead for a period of "dialogue."

Fidel has been forced to impose increasingly strict control over his people as he himself has grown old and weak, fainting in the sun during one of his lengthy speeches, breaking his leg in a pratfall from a stage (American television networks replayed the tape endlessly for laughs). But there is very little humor about life in Cuba. In 2003, Castro rounded up dissidents, poets, and theater people, and threw them in jail, sentencing many to long periods of hard labor. An international outcry ensued. Fidel wasn't listening.

Cubans are still attempting to flee their leader's island nightmare. Precisely like forty-five years ago, they board whatever will float, the latest creations being the boat-car, and are inevitably picked up by the U.S. Coast Guard. The refugees, in some but not all cases, are repatriated, provided the American government is fairly certain they will not be jailed or killed when they return.

And so it goes. Fidel Castro has outlasted them all, every single one of them, but he will, as he must, go the way of all flesh. His designated successor is his brother, Raúl. Some fear the repression will only continue; others anticipate with wide eyes an untouched Cuban market desperate for American investment, a Gap, a Starbucks, a McDonalds, on every corner in Havana. There has been a whiff of hope. In May of 2005, 365 independent groups seeking a transition from Castroism to democracy met in Cuba. Many of the visitors were detained, some were sent back to their countries of origin, a few were jailed. But the fact that Fidel allowed the meeting to take place at all is astonishing and must be taken as an encouraging sign.

Wait for it. It will come.

The United States government has remained far from blameless in all of this. A series of missteps has characterized American foreign policy toward Cuba ever since the Castro revolution, with economic sanctions and travel bans among the lowlights—all meant to somehow punish Fidel, all inevitably punishing the ordinary Cuban. The line today remains as hard as it was in 1960. American policy is one of nonengagement. An unnamed State Department official was unapologetic. "U.S. policy exists in the real world," he said, "with the cold, harsh fact of what Castro is and what he's done and continues to do to that country and the people in it."[8]

Castro has recently spawned an imitator in Venezuela: Hugo Chavez. Sweeping to power in 1998, Chavez spouted the virtues of the common man and almost immediately instituted a policy of class warfare, spending his country's oil millions on welfare programs for the poor, alienating Venezuela's business class, but doing oddly little to reduce the huge chasm between rich and poor there. He survived a brief coup in 2000 and has since consolidated his power in the legislative and executive branches. He has packed Venezuela's Supreme Court with his judges, expanding the bench from twenty to thirty-two seats.[9] He refused to let Venezuela's 2004 election be observed by European monitors; Chavez won amid widespread allegations of fraud. Chavez often appears before crowds in military regalia, like his hero Castro, who to this day dresses in fatigues. The only thing missing is the beard. Most recently, he has cracked down on political opponents, declaring the independent political group Sumate "enemies of the people." Sumate leader Maria Cornia Machado met with President George Bush in June 2005, a meeting whose very occurrence indicates that the United States wants Chavez to know somebody is paying attention. Like Castro, Chavez blames his country's problems on U.S. imperialism.

He has lately warned of a coming American invasion.

NOTES

THE SETUP

1. Hugh Thomas, *Rivers of Gold: The Rise of the Spanish Empire, from Columbus to Magellan* (New York: Random House, 2003), p. 77.
2. Ibid., p. 91.
3. Ibid., p. 53.
4. Ibid., p. 95.
5. Ibid., p. 435.
6. www.spanamwar.com: The Spanish American War Centennial Website, War in Cuba Background: The Cuban Revolution of 1895–98.
7. Hugh Thomas, *Cuba or the Pursuit of Freedom* (New York: Da Capo Press, 1998), p. 335.
8. Guantanamo Bay is turf we still have not surrendered. Guantanamo and the U.S. naval base there have been in and out of the headlines through coups, wars, revolutions, and counterrevolutions, but the American presence there has not budged since the Spanish-American war. Most recently, the United States has maintained the base as a way-station for Muslim and Arab enemy combatants rounded up during military action in Afghanistan, amid wild controversy over who these "combatants" are or were, why they are there, and when, if ever, they might either be brought to justice or allowed to leave.
9. Peggy Samuels and Harold Samuels, *Teddy Roosevelt at San Juan: The Making of a President* (College Station: Texas University Press, 1997), p. 10.
10. Ibid., p. 190.
11. Ibid., p. 230.
12. Ibid., p. 239.
13. Ibid., p. 285.
14. Hugh Thomas in *Cuba or the Pursuit of Freedom* makes the point that Cuba was a hot issue in the Cleveland-McKinley race of 1896.

15. www.floridahistory.org/floridians/1920s: Florida in the 1920s, "Binder Boys and Real Estate."
16. Warren Hinckle and William W. Turner, *The Fish Is Red: The Story of the Secret War Against Castro* (New York: Harper & Row, 1981), p. 46.
17. www.floridahistory.org/floridians/1920s: Florida in the 1920s, "The Hurricane of 1926."
18. Gay Talese, *Honor Thy Father* (New York: World Publishing, 1971), p. 185.
19. www.floridahistory.org/floridians/1920s: Florida in the 1920s, "Prohibition Days."
20. Bryan Burrough, *Public Enemies: America's Greatest Crime Wave and the Birth of the FBI, 1933–34* (New York: Penguin Press, 2004), p. 9.
21. Ibid., p. 35.
22. Thomas, *Cuba*, p. 502. The great historian also suggested that perhaps the country would have been better off if the United States completely took over for a while, then moved toward either genuine independence or outright annexation.
23. Thomas, *Cuba*, p. 504.
24. Ibid.
25. Ibid., pp. 569–70. Meanwhile, the Communist Party in Cuba organized. Labor was primarily influenced by the anarcho-syndicalists, but by the mid-1920s, left-wing thinking was alive with ideas imported by merchant seamen. The anarchists began to see the reasoning behind a party that could claim national organization and discipline. Joined by influential students, the Communists formed a single party in Havana in August 1925. The new group promptly adopted the principles coming out of Moscow, refusing, for example, to take part in any election. The Cuban Communists preached their doctrine to railway workers and stevedores. Their envoy to Moscow was an immigrant Polish Jew named Semjovich. Their uncertain ethnicity and small numbers (they totaled maybe one hundred in Havana) could have been reasons that the Cuban organization wasn't fully recognized by the Moscow-based Comintern, or International Communist Party, until 1928. Thomas, *Cuba*, pp. 577–78.
26. Ibid., p. 580.
27. Ibid., pp. 590–93.
28. Ibid., p. 607.
29. Ibid., p. 628.
30. Ibid., p. 645.
31. www.cuban-exile.com/doc_001–025/doc0016.html: Francis J. Sicius, *Cubans in Miami: An Historic Perspective*, p. 13.
32. Ibid., pp. 8–9.

33. Robert Lacey, *Little Man: Meyer Lansky and the Gangster Life* (Boston: Little, Brown, 1991), p. 85.
34. Ibid., pp. 116–17.
35. Ibid., p. 122.
36. Ibid., p. 735.
37. Thomas, *Cuba*, p. 737.
38. Tad Szulc, *Fidel: A Critical Portrait* (New York: Avon Books, 1987), pp. 173–76.
39. Jon Lee Anderson, *Che Guevara: A Revolutionary Life* (New York: Grove Press, 1997), pp. 175–77.
40. Leycester Coltman, *The Real Fidel Castro* (New Haven, CT: Yale University Press, 2003), p. 39.
41. Szulc, *Fidel: A Critical Portrait*, p. 175.
42. Ibid., p. 181.
43. Ibid., p. 183.
44. Thomas, *Cuba*, p. 758.
45. Ibid., p. 760.
46. Ibid., p. 776.
47. Ibid., p.785.

CHAPTER ONE

1. Author's interview with William P. Kelly, April 24, 2001.
2. J. Edgar Hoover, *Masters of Deceit: The Story of Communism in America and How to Fight It* (New York: Henry Holt, 1958), pp. v-vi.
3. Author's interview with William P. Kelly, April 2001.
4. Tad Szulc, *Fidel: A Critical Portrait* (New York: Avon Books, 1987), p. 226.
5. Ibid., pp. 238–39.
6. Leycester Coltman, *The Real Fidel Castro* (New Haven, CT: Yale University Press, 2003), p. 72.
7. Szulc, *Fidel: A Critical Portrait*, p. 243.
8. Coltman, *The Real Fidel Castro*, p. 74.
9. Ibid., p. 77.
10. Hugh Thomas, *Cuba or the Pursuit of Freedom* (New York: Da Capo Press, 1998), p. 837.
11. Coltman, *The Real Fidel Castro*, p. 81, pp. 82–83.
12. Ibid., p. 86
13. Szulc, *Fidel: A Critical Portrait*, p. 310.
14. Ibid., p. 320.
15. Stephen E. Ambrose, *Rise to Globalism: American Foreign Policy Since 1938* (New York: Penguin Books, 1991), p. 175.

16. Robert Lacey, *Little Man: Meyer Lansky and the Gangster Life* (Boston: Little, Brown, 1991), p. 226.
17. Ibid., p. 247.
18. David Halberstam, *The Fifties* (New York: Villard Books, 1993), p. 714.
19. Lacey, *Little Man*, p. 231; Halberstam, *The Fifties*, p. 714.
20. Halberstam, *The Fifties*, pp. 714–15.
21. Jon Lee Anderson, *Che Guevara: A Revolutionary Life* (New York: Grove Press, 1997), p. 160.
22. Ibid., p. 114.
23. Szulc, *Fidel: A Critical Portrait*, p. 342.
24. Coltman, *The Real Fidel Castro*, p. 99.
25. Anderson, *Che Guevara*, pp. 172–73.
26. Ibid., pp. 203–4.
27. Ibid., p. 207, p. 212.
28. Ibid., p. 212.
29. Ibid., pp. 213–14. With an asterisk Anderson notes on page 213: "The exact figure of *Granma* survivors has remained imprecise. Official accounts have always referred to the number who survived and regrouped to form the core of the rebel army as twelve. The figure, with its unabashed apostolic symbolism, was consecrated by the revolutionary Cuban journalist and official historian Carlos Franqui in his book *Los Doce* (The Twelve). Like many other early supporters, Franqui later went into exile as an opponent of Castro."
30. Ibid., p. 218.
31. Thomas, *Cuba*, p. 910.
32. "Rebel Strength Gaining in Cuba, But Batista Has the Upper Hand," *New York Times*, February 25, 1957.
33. Ibid.
34. Thomas, *Cuba*, p. 919.
35. Szulc, *Fidel: A Critical Portrait*, p.445.
36. Anderson, *Che Guevara*, p. 236.
37. Wayne S. Smith, *The Closest of Enemies* (New York: W. W. Norton, 1987), p.16.
38. Ibid., p. 17.
39. Ibid., p. 27.
40. Howard Hunt, *Give Us This Day* (New Rochelle, NY: Arlington House, 1973), p. 91.
41. Smith, *The Closest of Enemies*, p. 19.
42. Ambrose, *Rise to Globalism*, p. 132.
43. Halberstam, *The Fifties*, p. 56.
44. Ambrose, *Rise to Globalism*, pp. 134–35.
45. Smith, *The Closest of Enemies*, p. 49.

46. Ibid., p. 21.
47. Ibid., p. 25.
48. Thomas, *Cuba*, p. 1014, p. 1018, p. 1019.
49. Testimony of Santo Trafficante before the House Select Committee on Assassinations (HSCA), September 28, 1978.
50. Ibid.
51. Lacey, *Little Man*, p. 252.
52. Lewis Yablonsky, *George Raft* (San Francisco: Mercury House, 1974), p. 204.
53. Ibid., pp. 205–06.
54. Peter Valenti, *Errol Flynn: A Bio-Bibliography* (Westport, CT: Greenwood Press, 1984), pp. 50–51.
55. Jeffrey Meyers, *Inherited Risk: Errol and Sean Flynn in Hollywood and Vietnam* (New York: Simon & Schuster, 2002), p. 289.
56. Smith, *The Closest of Enemies*, p. 37.
57. Meyers, *Inherited Risk*, p. 291.
58. Valenti, *Errol Flynn*, pp. 94–95.
59. Smith, *The Closest of Enemies*, p. 38.
60. Valenti, *Errol Flynn*, p. 54.
61. Testimony of Santo Trafficante, HSOA.
62. Yablonsky, *George Raft*, p. 221.
63. Smith, *The Closest of Enemies*, p. 38.

CHAPTER TWO

1. "Looters Axes Sound Knell of Cuba Gambling," Associated Press; *New York Journal-American*, January 4, 1959.
2. Lewis Yablonsky, *George Raft* (San Francisco: Mercury House, 1974), p. 221.
3. Wayne S. Smith, *The Closest of Enemies* (New York: W. W. Norton, 1987), p. 40; Robert Lacey repeats the account in *Little Man: Meyer Lansky and the Gangster Life* (Boston: Little, Brown, 1991), p. 258.
4. Yablonsky, *George Raft*, p. 221.
5. "Raft Not Natural After Cuba 'Fade'," *Miami Herald*, January 9, 1959.
6. "Safe in Cuba, Raft Reports," *New York Journal-American*, January 6, 1959.
7. Yablonsky, *George Raft*, p. 225.
8. "Raft Not Natural After Cuba 'Fade'," *Miami Herald*, January 9, 1959.
9. Yablonsky, *George Raft*, p. 225.
10. "Raft Not Natural After Cuba Fade," *Miami Herald*, January 9, 1959.
11. Jeffrey Meyers, *Inherited Risk: Errol and Sean Flynn in Hollywood and Vietnam* (New York: Simon & Schuster, 2002), p. 260.

12. "Flynn Says He Fought With Fidel," Associated Press, January 6, 1959.
13. "Errol Shot in Leg While With Castro," United Press International, January 6, 1959.
14. "Miami's Airport Provides Brief Skirmish of Cubans," *Miami Herald*, January 2, 1959.
15. "Chief Headley's Wise Decision," *Miami Herald*, January 9, 1959.
16. Testimony of Santo Trafficante before the House Select Committee on Assassinations (HSCA), September 28, 1978.
17. "Havana Gamblers Fleeing to U.S.," *Miami Herald*, January 2, 1959.
18. Lacey, *Little Man*, pp. 251–52.
19. "Cuba the Mob is Back," *Time*, March 2, 1959.
20. Testimony of Santo Trafficante, HSCA, September 28, 1978.
21. "Firm Hands On The Reins," *Miami Herald*, January 7, 1959.
22. "Recognizing The New Cuba," *Miami Herald*, January 9, 1959.
23. Meyers, *Inherited Risk*, p. 291.
24. "Firm Hands On the Reins," *Miami Herald*, January 7, 1959.
25. Stephen E. Ambrose, *Rise to Globalism: American Foreign Policy Since 1938* (New York: Penguin Books, 1991), p. 175.
26. "Gambling Headache To All Concerned," *Miami Herald*, January 7, 1959.
27. "Cuba, Castro and the Casinos," *Newsweek*, March 2, 1959.
28. "Cuba One Man Court," *Time*, March 14, 1959.
29. Jon Lee Anderson, *Che Guevara: A Revolutionary Life* (New York: Grove Press, 1997), p. 257.
30. Ibid., pp. 385–86. To this day, Guevara apologists gloss over, rationalize, or ignore the fact that Che's actions were the equivalent of mass murder, a fact that has yet to be squared with his ubiquitous popular image.
31. Ibid., p. 389.
32. "Cuba, Another Guatemala?," *Newsweek*, April 13, 1959.
33. David Halberstam, *The Fifties* (New York: Villard Books, 1993), p. 721.
34. Ambrose, *Rise to Globalism*, p. 176.
35. Smith, *The Closest of Enemies*, p. 48.
36. Author's interview with E. Howard Hunt, December 6, 2003.
37. Author's interview with William P. Kelly, April 24, 2001.
38. Author's interview with William Holloman, June 2001.
39. "Red Weed Grows in Cuba," *Miami News*, April 26, 1959.
40. Author's interview with William P. Kelly, April 24, 2001.
41. Ibid.
42. "Bearded Latin Wins Over Capital," Associated Press, April 21, 1959.
43. Ibid.

44. "Red Weed Grows in Cuba," *Miami News,* April 26, 1959.
45. Ibid.
46. "Castro, Key Men Linked to Reds," *Miami News,* April 26, 1959.
47. "Live It Up is Fidel's N.Y. Pace," United Press International, April 24, 1959.
48. "Nab Crank with Bomb Near Castro During Talk," *New York World Telegram and Sun,* April 25, 1959.
49. "How 'Bomber' Was Caught," *New York Post,* April 26, 1959.
50. "Nab Crank with Bomb Near Castro During Talk," *New York World Telegram and Sun,* April 25, 1959.
51. "How 'Bomber' Was Caught," *New York Post,* April 26, 1959.
52. "Nab Crank with Bomb Near Castro During Talk," *New York World Telegram and Sun,* April 25, 1959.
53. "How 'Bomber' Was Caught," *New York Post,* April 26, 1959.

CHAPTER THREE

1. Robert Lacey, *Little Man: Meyer Lansky and the Gangster Life* (Boston: Little, Brown, 1991), p. 254.
2. Ibid., pp. 254–255.
3. Testimony of Santo Trafficante before the House Select Committee on Assassinations (HSCA), September 28, 1978.
4. Jeffrey Meyers, *Inherited Risk: Errol and Sean Flynn in Hollywood and Vietnam* (New York: Simon & Schuster, 2002), pp. 291–92.
5. Hugh Thomas, *Cuba or the Pursuit of Freedom* (New York: Da Capo Press, 1998), p. 1075.
6. FBI Memo, Bureau File #2–1573, May 9, 1960.
7. Ibid.
8. FBI Memo from J. Edgar Hoover, December 11, 1959.
9. Ibid.
10. "Invasion of Cuba Called Imminent," *New York Times,* December 29, 1959.
11. FBI Memo, New York, December 14, 1959.
12. "Honduras Denies Charges," AP, December 28, 1959.
13. FBI Report #NY2–554, no date.
14. FBI Bureau File # 2–1573, February 5, 1960.
15. FBI Memorandum from F. J. Baumgardner to Mr. Belmont, December 15, 1959.
16. Letter from J. Edgar Hoover to New York Special Agent in Charge, January 18, 1960.
17. Author's interview with William Holloman, June 2001.
18. FBI Interview Report #NY 2–554, New York, January 25, 1960.

19. FBI Report #JK 2–11, February 1, 1960.
20. FBI Field Office File #2–237, Miami, February 5, 1960.
21. Ibid.
22. FBI Report, Field Office File#2–237, Bureau File # 2–1573, Miami, March 30, 1960.
23. FBI Report #MM2–237, 2–1573, Miami, May 9, 1960. The vessel cited is an ASR–63, an air-sea rescue boat. This could be the "yacht" that Thomas refers to on p.1275 of *Cuba*.
24. FBI Memo from F. J. Baumgardner, April 22, 1960.

CHAPTER FOUR

1. Robert Dallek, *An Unfinished Life: John F. Kennedy, 1917–1963* (New York: Back Bay Books/Little, Brown, 2004), pp. 235–36.
2. Ibid., p. 244.
3. Hugh Thomas, *Cuba or the Pursuit of Freedom* (New York: Da Capo Press, 1998), p. 1269.
4. David Halberstam, *The Fifties* (New York: Villard Books, 1993), p. 724.
5. Thomas, *Cuba*, p. 1269.
6. Halberstam, *The Fifties*, p. 725.
7. Thomas, *Cuba*, p. 1272.
8. Wayne S. Smith, *The Closest of Enemies* (New York: W. W. Norton, 1987), p. 36.
9. Howard Hunt, *Give Us This Day* (New Rochelle, NY: Arlington House, 1973), p. 90.
10. Halberstam, *The Fifties*, p. 725.
11. Smith, *The Closest of Enemies*, p. 58.
12. Ibid., p. 60.
13. Ibid., p. 61.
14. Peter Kornbluth, ed., *Bay of Pigs Declassified: The Secret CIA Report on the Invasion of Cuba* (New York: New Press, 1998), p. 24.
15. Author's interview with E. Howard Hunt, December 6, 2003.
16. Howard Hunt, *Give Us This Day*, p. 29.
17. Ibid., p. 32.
18. Ibid., pp. 33–34.
19. Ibid., p. 36.
20. "U.S.-Cuban Relations: Battleground, U.S.A.," *Newsweek*, October 31, 1960.
21. "Exiles Stage Protest To Nik's Cuba Visit," *Miami Herald*, June 5, 1960.
22. "U.S.-Cuban Relations: Battleground, U.S.A.," *Newsweek*, October 31, 1960.

23. Ibid.
24. Author's interview with William P. Kelly, April 24, 2001.
25. "U.S.-Cuban Relations: Battleground, U.S.A.," *Newsweek,* October 31, 1960.
26. "Time To Challenge Castro?," *Miami Herald,* June 7, 1960.
27. "Cuba Boots Two Embassy Employees," Associated Press, June 16, 1960.
28. "A Day For Insults: Cuba Expels Two Yanks," *Miami News,* June 16, 1960.
29. FBI Memorandum, Special Agent Sweet to Mr. Belmont, June 18, 1960.
30. Author's interview with E. Howard Hunt, December 6, 2003.
31. FBI Memorandum, Special Agent Sweet to Mr. Belmont, June 18, 1960.
32. Telegram from Legat, Havana, to Director. June 16, 1960.
33. FBI Memo from Special Agent in Charge, Miami to Director, FBI, Bureau File #MM 66–2698, June 16, 1960.
34. State Department Telegram no.3614, June 16, 1960, 11 A.M.
35. "A Day for Insults: Cuba Expels Two Yanks," *Miami News,* June 16, 1960.
36. Telegram no. 222 Legat, Havana, to Director, FBI, June 16, 1960.
37. "A Day for Insults: Cuba Expels Two Yanks," *Miami News,* June 16, 1960.
38. FBI Memo, Bureau File #MM 66–2608, June 16, 1960.
39. FBI Memo from Alan Belmont to Parsons, et al., June 16, 1960.
40. FBI Memo from Alan Belmont to Parsons, et al., also dated June 16, 1960.
41. FBI Memo from Alan Belmont to Parsons, et al., June 17, 1960.
42. FBI Memo from Special Agent Sweet to Alan Belmont, June 20, 1960.

CHAPTER FIVE

1. Retired FBI assistant director Edwin Sharp said that the bureau, as a matter of policy, was advising suspects of their rights long before *Miranda* became the law of the land. Author's interview with Edwin Sharp, September 1, 2005.
2. Author's interview with William P. Kelly, April 24, 2001.
3. Author's interview with William Holloman, June 2001.
4. Ibid.
5. "Castro Fall Before 1961-Ellender," *Miami News,* June 22, 1960.

6. Hugh Thomas, *Cuba or the Pursuit of Freedom* (New York: Da Capo Press, 1998), p. 1230.
7. Warren Hinckle and William W. Turner, *The Fish Is Red: The Story of the Secret War Against Castro* (New York: Harper & Row, 1981), p. 52. Sturgis, under the guidance and direction of E. Howard Hunt, would later be convicted as a coconspirator in the Watergate break-in.
8. Author's interview with William Holloman, June, 2001.
9. "Cuban 'Army' Broken Up," *Miami News*, June 22, 1960.
10. "Recruit Tells How Anti-Castro 'Army' Came to Grief," *Miami Herald*, June 24, 1960.
11. Ibid.
12. "How The Doughnut Army Hit at Cuba," *Miami News*, June 24, 1960.
13. Ibid.
14. "Recruit Tells How Anti-Castro 'Army' Came to Grief," *Miami Herald*, June 24, 1960.
15. Ibid.
16. "How the Doughnut Army Hit at Cuba," *Miami News*, June 24, 1960.
17. Ibid.
18. Ibid.
19. "Recruit Tells How Anti-Castro 'Army' Came to Grief," *Miami Herald*, June 24, 1960.
20. "How the Doughnut Army Hit at Cuba," *Miami News*, June 24, 1960.
21. "Recruit Tells How Anti-Castro 'Army' Came to Grief," *Miami Herald*, June 24, 1960.
22. Author's interview with William P. Kelly, April 24, 2001.
23. "How the Doughnut Army Hit at Cuba " *Miami News*, June 24, 1960.
24. Author's interview with William P. Kelly, April 24, 2001.
25. "Did Fidel Plot U.S. Scheme?," *Miami News*, June 23, 1960.
26. Howard Hunt, *Give Us This Day* (New Rochelle, NY: Arlington House, 1973), p. 104.
27. "Did Fidel Plot U.S. Scheme?," *Miami News*, June 23, 1960.
28. "Recruit Tells How Anti-Castro 'Army' Came to Grief," *Miami Herald*, June 24, 1960.

CHAPTER SIX

1. Stephen E. Ambrose, *Rise to Globalism: American Foreign Policy Since 1938* (New York: Penguin Books, 1991), p. 153.
2. Ibid., p. 154.
3. Author's interview with E. Howard Hunt, December 6, 2003.
4. Warren Hinckle and William W. Turner, *The Fish Is Red: The Story of the Secret War Against Castro* (New York: Harper & Row, 1981), p. 41.

5. Author's interview with E. Howard Hunt, December 6, 2003.

6. Ambrose, *Rise to Globalism*, p. 155.

7. Author's interview with E. Howard Hunt, December 6, 2003.

8. Peter Wyden, *Bay of Pigs: The Untold Story* (New York: Simon & Schuster, 1979), p. 15.

9. Evan Thomas, *The Very Best Men: Four Who Dared, the Early Years of the CIA* (New York: Touchstone Books / Simon & Schuster, 1996), p. 94.

10. Wyden, *Bay of Pigs*, p. 21.

11. Haynes Johnson, *The Bay of Pigs: The Leaders' Story of Brigade 2506* (New York: W. W. Norton, 1964), p. 26.

12. Author's interview with E. Howard Hunt. Bernie Barker gained later infamy as a Watergate burglar.

13. Johnson, *The Bay of Pigs*, p. 26.

14. Ibid., pp. 26–27.

15. Howard Hunt, *Give Us This Day* (New Rochelle, NY: Arlington House, 1973), p. 47.

16. Johnson, *The Bay of Pigs*, pp. 29–30.

17. Wyden, *Bay of Pigs*, p. 32.

18. Ibid., p. 33.

19. Author's interview with E. Howard Hunt, December 6, 2003.

20. Hunt, *Give Us This Day*, p. 46.

21. Ibid., p. 50.

22. Johnson, *The Bay of Pigs*, pp. 32–33.

23. Ibid., pp. 37–38.

24. Ibid., pp. 41–42.

25. Ibid., p. 44.

26. Ibid., p. 37.

27. Ibid., p. 56.

28. Robert Dallek, *An Unfinished Life: John F. Kennedy, 1917–1963* (New York: Back Bay Books / Little, Brown, 2004), p. 247.

29. Ibid., p. 265.

30. Ibid., p. 266. Contrast the breathless excitement of that 1960 Democratic convention with what we have over forty years later. A front runner is established after one or two primary wins, the speechifying pays homage to various tried and true "positions" and the candidate is crowned.

31. Ibid., p. 279.

32. Author's interview with William P. Kelly, April 24, 2001.

33. Wyden, *Bay of Pigs*, pp. 39–40.

34. Ibid., pp. 40–41.

35. Charles Rappleye and Ed Becker, *All American Mafioso: The Johnny Rosselli Story* (New York: Doubleday, 1991), p. 181.

36. Wyden, *Bay of Pigs,* p. 41.
37. Rappleye and Becker, *All American Mafioso,* p. 24.
38. Ibid., p. 27.
39. Ibid., p. 30.
40. Ibid., p. 46.
41. Ibid., p. 53.
42. Ibid., pp. 82–83.
43. Ron Lebrecque, unpublished interview with Jimmy "The Weasel" Frattiano, Salt Lake City, November 7, 1981.
44. Ibid.
45. Rappleye and Becker, *All American Mafioso,* p. 146.
46. Ibid., pp. 184–85.
47. Wyden, *Bay of Pigs,* p. 41.
48. Ibid.
49. Hinckle and Turner, *The Fish Is Red,* p. 29.
50. Wyden, *Bay of Pigs,* p. 42.

CHAPTER SEVEN

1. William Taubman, *Khrushchev: The Man and His Era* (New York: W. W. Norton, 2003), p. 474.
2. Ibid., p. 475.
3. David Halberstam, *The Fifties* (New York: Villard Books, 1993), p. 702.
4. Taubman, *Khrushchev,* p. 475.
5. Ibid., pp. 475–76.
6. "Castro Stays in Room; Hotel Praises Conduct," *New York Herald-Tribune,* September 26, 1960
7. Author's interview with Kevin Tierney, April 23, 2003.
8. "Castro Stays in Room; Hotel Praises Conduct," *New York Herald-Tribune,* September 26, 1960.
9. Taubman, *Khrushchev,* p.475.
10. Author's interview with Kevin Tierney, April 23, 2003.
11. Robert Kaplan, *Balkan Ghosts* (New York: Vintage Departures, 1994), p. 14.
12. Author's interview with Kevin Tierney, April 23, 2003.
13. Warren Hinckle and William W. Turner, *The Fish Is Red: The Story of the Secret War Against Castro* (New York: Harper & Row, 1981), p. 30.
14. Undated and unsigned CIA field memorandum.
15. "Barmaid Says 'Hook' Warned Her to Leave," *New York Mirror,* March 7, 1961.
16. "2 Are Shot Here As Cubans Clash," *New York Times,* September 22, 1960.

17. "Barmaid Says 'Hook' Warned Her To Leave," *New York Mirror*, March 7, 1961.
18. "The Most Innocent Bystander," *Master Detective*, February 1961.
19. "Girl, 9, And Man Shot in Castro Tavern Riot," *New York Daily News*, September 22, 1960.
20. "The Most Innocent Bystander," *Master Detective*, February 1961.
21. "Barmaid Says 'Hook' Warned Her To Leave," *New York Mirror*, March 7, 1961.
22. "Girl, 9, and Man Shot in Castro Tavern Riot," *New York Daily News*, September 22, 1960.
23. "The Most Innocent Bystander," *Master Detective*, February 1961.
24. Ibid.
25. Ibid.
26. Ibid.
27. "Cops Take Weapons from 3 at Fidel Fete," *New York Daily News*, September 23,
28. "The Most Innocent Bystander," *Master Detective*, February 1961.
29. Ibid.
30. "FBI Joins in Search for Girl's 1-Arm Killer," *New York Mirror*, September 23, 1960.
31. "The Most Innocent Bystander," *Master Detective*, February 1961.
32. "Cops Take Weapons from 3 at Fidel Fete," *New York Daily News*, September 23, 1960.
33. "The Most Innocent Bystander," *Master Detective*, February 1961.
34. "FBI Joins in Search For Girl's 1-Arm Killer," *New York Mirror*, September 23, 1960.
35. "FBI Out To Capture Cuba Thug," Associated Press, September 27, 1960.
36. Author's interview with William P. Kelly, April 24, 2001.
37. "The Most Innocent Bystander," *Master Detective*, February 1961.
38. "The Hook Seized in Child's Death," *New York Daily News*, October 15, 1960.
39. "'Hook' Seized in Killing of Girl, 9," *New York Herald-Tribune*, October 15, 1960.
40. "The Most Innocent Bystander," *Master Detective*, February 1961.
41. "'Hook' Seized in Killing of Girl, 9," *New York Herald-Tribune*, October 15, 1960.
42. "The Hook Seized in Child's Death," *New York Daily News*, October 15, 1960.
43. "'Hook' Seized in Killing of Girl, 9," *New York Herald-Tribune*, October 15, 1960.
44. Undated and unsigned CIA field memorandum.

45.   "'Hook' Seized in Killing of Girl, 9," *New York Herald-Tribune,* October 15, 1960.

46.   "The Hook Seized in Child's Death," *New York Daily News,* October 15, 1960.

CHAPTER EIGHT

1.   Robert Dallek, *An Unfinished Life: John F. Kennedy, 1917–1963* (New York: Back Bay Books / Little, Brown, 2004), pp. 284–85.

2.   "Johnson Blames 'Cuban Mess' on Republicans," United Press International, October 14, 1960.

3.   David Halberstam, *The Fifties* (New York: Villard Books, 1993), p. 700.

4.   Ibid., pp. 728–29.

5.   Ibid., p. 729.

6.   Peter Wyden, *Bay of Pigs: The Untold Story* (New York: Simon & Schuster, 1979), p. 28.

7.   Dallek, *An Unfinished Life* p. 290.

8.   Wyden, *Bay of Pigs,* p. 43.

9.   Ibid., pp. 43–44.

10.   Sam Giancana and Chuck Giancana, *Double Cross* (New York: Warner Books, 1992), p. 30.

11.   Ibid., p. 71.

12.   Testimony of Santo Trafficante before the House Select Committee on Assassinations (HSCA), September 28, 1978.

13.   Ibid.

14.   Giancana and Giancana, *Double Cross,* p. 51.

15.   Wyden, *Bay of Pigs,* p. 41.

16.   Charles Rappleye and Ed Becker, *All American Mafioso: The Johnny Rosselli Story* (New York: Doubleday, 1991), p.190.

17.   Testimony of Santo Trafficante before the House Select Committee on Assassinations (HSCA), September 28, 1978.

18.   Giancana and Giancana, *Double Cross,* p. 408.

19.   Testimony of Santo Trafficante before the House Select Committee on Assassinations (HSCA), September 28, 1978.

20.   Warren Hinckle and William W. Turner, *The Fish Is Red: The Story of the Secret War Against Castro* (New York: Harper & Row, 1981), p. 38.

21.   Wyden, *Bay of Pigs,* p. 44.

22.   Hinckle and Turner, *The Fish Is Red,* p. 38.

23.   Ron Lebrecque, unpublished interview with Jimmy "The Weasel" Frattiano, Salt Lake City, November 7, 1981.

24.   Wyden, *Bay of Pigs,* p. 44.

25.   Halberstam, *The Fifties,* p. 728.

26. Wyden, *Bay of Pigs*, p. 45.
27. Ibid., p. 46.
28. Author's interview with William P. Kelly, April 24, 2001.
29. Author's interview with E. Howard Hunt, December 6, 2003.
30. CIA Memorandum for the record, May 18, 1961.
31. Author's interview with William Holloman, June 2001.
32. Ibid.

CHAPTER NINE

1. Stephen E. Ambrose, *Rise to Globalism: American Foreign Policy Since 1938* (New York: Penguin Books, 1991), p. 179.
2. Warren Hinckle and William W. Turner, *The Fish Is Red: The Story of the Secret War Against Castro* (New York: Harper & Row, 1981), p.39.
3. Ambrose, *Rise to Globalism*, p. 180.
4. Hugh Thomas, *Cuba or the Pursuit of Freedom* (New York: Da Capo Press, 1998), p. 1283.
5. Howard Hunt, *Give Us This Day* (New Rochelle, NY: Arlington House, 1973), p. 71.
6. Robert Dallek, *An Unfinished Life: John F. Kennedy, 1917–1963* (New York: Back Bay Books/Little, Brown, 2004), p. 293–94.
7. "Are We Training Cuban Guerrillas?," *Nation*, November 19, 1960.
8. Hinckle and Turner, *The Fish Is Red*, p.68. The *New York Times* eventually did run a story however, on January 10, 1961, as Peter Wyden points out on page 46 of *Bay of Pigs*. Nobody cared.
9. The *Nation*, whose paleoliberal slant has remained ossified for the better part of a century, can be forgiven its idealism. Hinckle and Turner, a hardened investigative journalist and an FBI man, respectively, cannot. The problem is that Hinckle and Turner are Vietnam-era to their core (their book was published in 1982) and their retrograde hope appears to be that an informed populace enlightened by the mighty *New York Times* would have taken to the streets in righteous indignation and put a stop to this march to military folly. But 1960 was not 1968. America was a very different country.
10. Dallek, *An Unfinished Life*, p. 315.
11. Ibid., p. 358.
12. Hinckle and Turner, *The Fish Is Red*, p. 61.
13. Hunt, *Give Us This Day*, p. 56.
14. Haynes Johnson, *The Bay of Pigs: The Leaders' Story of Brigade 2506* (New York: W. W. Norton, 1964), p.47.
15. Hunt, *Give Us This Day*, p. 127.
16. Ibid., p. 129.

17. Ibid., p. 133.
18. Ibid., p.134.
19. Ibid., p. 150.
20. Peter Wyden, *Bay of Pigs: The Untold Story* (New York: Simon & Schuster, 1979), p. 100.
21. Ibid., p. 114.
22. Ibid.
23. Hunt, *Give Us This Day,* p. 92.
24. Ibid., p. 94.
25. Ibid., p. 175.
26. Wyden, *Bay of Pigs,* p. 116.
27. Hunt, *Give Us This Day,* p. 182.
28. Ibid., p. 160.
29. Hinckle and Turner, *The Fish Is Red,* p. 73.
30. Ibid. Santo later denied everything. "I didn't receive no pills from Rosselli, and I don't know what else to say about that." Testimony before the House Select Committee on Assassinations, September 28, 1978.
31. Charles Rappleye and Ed Becker, *All American Mafioso: The Johnny Rosselli Story* (New York: Doubleday, 1991), pp. 191–92.
32. Hinckle and Turner, *The Fish Is Red,* p. 76.
33. Dallek, *An Unfinished Life,* p. 360.
34. Wyden, *Bay of Pigs,* p. 122.
35. Ibid., p. 121.
36. Ibid., p. 122.
37. "Molina Is Guilty in Girl's Slaying," *New York Times,* April 8, 1961.
38. Author's interview with William P. Kelly, April 24, 2001.
39. "Molina Is Guilty in Girls' Slaying," *New York Times,* April 8, 1961.
40. Hinckle and Turner, *The Fish Is Red,* p. 82.

CHAPTER TEN

1. In his book *Give Us This Day* (New Rochelle, NY: Arlington House, 1973), Howard Hunt wrote, "a mass popular uprising had never been expected or contemplated" (p. 201). Subsequent testimony by Richard Bissell and Allen Dulles corroborate this information, but whether this was, in fact, true or was a matter of face-saving in the wake of disaster has always been a point of hot contention.
2. Warren Hinckle and William W. Turner, *The Fish Is Red: The Story of the Secret War Against Castro* (New York: Harper & Row, 1981), p. 84.
3. Hunt, *Give Us This Day,* p. 193.
4. Hinckle and Turner, *The Fish Is Red,* pp. 85–86.
5. Ibid., p. 86.

6. Peter Kornbluth, ed., *Bay of Pigs Declassified: The Secret CIA Report on the Invasion of Cuba* (New York: New Press, 1998), p. 306.

7. Ibid.

8. Hunt, *Give Us This Day,* p. 195.

9. Ibid., p. 196.

10. Hinckle and Turner, *The Fish Is Red,* p. 87.

11. Hunt, *Give Us This Day,* p. 197.

12. Robert Dallek, *An Unfinished Life: John F. Kennedy, 1917–1963* (New York: Back Bay Books/Little, Brown, 2004), p. 364. In his discussion of the critical hours of April 16 and 17, Dallek cavalierly dismisses the crucial necessity of that second air strike, and by doing so, reinforces one of the longstanding myths so dear to Kennedy apologists. There is no getting around how damaging Kennedy's refusal to order the second strike—or series of strikes, or while they were at it, continued strikes—was to the efforts of Brigade 2506. Finally, this line of thinking assumes that even if the planes had been ordered in, everything else would have gone precisely the same—a ludicrous assumption.

13. Peter Wyden, *Bay of Pigs: The Untold Story* (New York: Simon & Schuster, 1979), pp. 218–19.

14. Ibid., p. 221.

15. Hunt, *Give Us This Day,* pp. 184–85. It would have been interesting to see how the Cuba Project's leaders would have reacted had Ray decided to leave.

16. Kornbluth, *Bay of Pigs Declassified,* pp. 307–08.

17. Haynes Johnson, *The Bay of Pigs: The Leaders' Story of Brigade 2506* (New York: W. W. Norton, 1964), p. 111.

18. Wyden, *Bay of Pigs,* p. 229.

19. Kornbluth, *Bay of Pigs Declassified,* p. 310.

20. Johnson, *The Bay of Pigs,* p. 125.

21. Ibid.

22. Hinckle and Turner, *The Fish Is Red,* p. 90.

23. Hunt, *Give Us This Day,* p. 207.

24. Johnson, *The Bay of Pigs,* p. 135.

25. Ibid., p. 143.

26. Dallek, *An Unfinished Life,* p. 365. Like some Gilded Age swell touring a turn of the twentieth-century slum, JFK in his patrician finery presided over an unmitigated disaster. The only thing missing from Dallek's retelling is a cigar, which, in fact, Kennedy was quite fond of smoking.

27. Ibid., pp. 366–67.

28. Ibid., pp. 367–68.

29. Johnson, *The Bay of Pigs,* p. 160.

30. Kornbluth, *Bay of Pigs Declassified*, p.319. Haynes Johnson and Howard Hunt have this message ending in "the woods"; Hinckle and Turner's version says "the swamps."
31. Wyden, *Bay of Pigs*, pp. 291–92.
32. Joan Didion, *Miami* (New York: Simon & Schuster, 1987), p.168.
33. Hunt, *Give Us This Day*, p. 210.
34. Johnson, *The Bay of Pigs*, pp. 181–82.
35. Ibid., p. 186.
36. Ibid., p. 187.
37. Ibid., pp. 188–89.
38. Wyden, *Bay of Pigs*, pp. 298–99.
39. Ibid., pp. 299–300.
40. Tad Szulc, *Fidel: A Critical Portrait* (New York: Avon Books, 1987), pp. 615–16.
41. "No Tractor Swap for 3, Says Castro," United Press International, June 14, 1961.
42. "The Hook Gets 20 Yrs. to Life," *New York Mirror*, June 30, 1961.
43. CIA Memorandum for the record, May 5, 1964. MORI DocID 277756.
44. Wyden, *Bay of Pigs*, p. 303.
45. Ibid.

EPILOGUE

1. Joan Didion, *Miami* (New York: Simon & Schuster, 1987), pp. 19–20.
2. Author's interview with William P. Kelly, April 24, 2001.
3. Robert Lacey, *Little Man: Meyer Lansky and the Gangster Life* (Boston: Little, Brown, 1991), p. 414.
4. Jon Lee Anderson, *Che Guevara: A Revolutionary Life* (New York: Grove Press, 1997), p. 716.
5. Ibid., p. 737.
6. Ibid., p. 739.
7. http://cubanet.org//CNews/y00/apr00/17e10.htm: "Cuban Army Seen as Key to Ouster of Castro."
8. Europeans Capitulate In Showdown On Cuba," *New York Sun*, June 14, 2005.
9. "Americas," *Wall Street Journal*, June 10, 2005.

BIBLIOGRAPHY

Ambrose, Stephen E. *Rise to Globalism: American Foreign Policy Since 1938.* 6th rev. ed. New York: Penguin Books, 1991.

Anderson, Jon Lee. *Che Guevara: A Revolutionary Life.* New York: Grove Press, 1997.

Barron, John. *Operation Solo: The FBI's Man in the Kremlin.* Washington, D.C.: Regnery Publishing, 1996.

Burrough, Bryan. *Public Enemies: America's Greatest Crime Wave and the Birth of the FBI, 1933–34.* New York: Penguin Press, 2004.

Coltman, Leycester. *The Real Fidel Castro.* New Haven, CT: Yale University Press, 2003.

Dallek, Robert. *An Unfinished Life: John F. Kennedy, 1917–1963.* New York: Back Bay Books/Little, Brown, 2004.

Didion, Joan. *Miami.* New York: Simon & Schuster, 1987.

Ellroy, James. *American Tabloid.* New York: Alfred A Knopf, 1995.

Giancana, Sam, and Chuck Giancana. *Double Cross.* New York: Warner Books, 1992.

Halberstam, David. *The Fifties.* New York: Villard Books, 1993.

Hinckle, Warren, and William W. Turner. *The Fish Is Red: The Story of the Secret War Against Castro.* New York: Harper & Row, 1981.

Hoover, J. Edgar. *Masters of Deceit: The Story of Communism in America and How to Fight It.* New York: Henry Holt, 1958.

Hunt, Howard. *Give Us This Day.* New Rochelle, NY: Arlington House, 1973.

Johnson, Haynes. *The Bay of Pigs: The Leaders' Story of Brigade 2506.* New York: W. W. Norton, 1964.

Kaplan, Robert. *Balkan Ghosts: A Journey Through History.* New York: Vintage Departures, 1994.

Keller, Gary D. and Cordelia Candelaria, eds. *The Legacy of the Mexican and Spanish American Wars: Legal, Literary, and Historical Perspectives.* Tempe, AZ: Bilingual Press, 2000.

Kornbluth, Peter, ed. *Bay of Pigs Declassified: The Secret CIA Report on the Invasion of Cuba.* New York: New Press, 1998.

Lacey, Robert. *Little Man: Meyer Lansky and the Gangster Life.* Boston: Little, Brown, 1991.

Meyers, Jeffrey. *Inherited Risk: Errol and Sean Flynn in Hollywood and Vietnam.* New York: Simon & Schuster, 2002.

Rappleye, Charles, and Ed Becker. *All American Mafioso: The Johnny Rosselli Story.* New York: Doubleday, 1991.

Samuels, Peggy, and Harold Samuels. *Teddy Roosevelt at San Juan: The Making of a President.* College Station: Texas University Press, 1997.

Smith, Wayne S. *The Closest of Enemies.* New York: W. W. Norton, 1987.

Szulc, Tad. *Fidel: A Critical Portrait.* New York: Avon Books, 1987.

Talese, Gay. *Honor Thy Father.* New York: World Publishing/Times Mirror, 1971.

Taubman, William. *Khrushchev: The Man and His Era.* New York: W. W. Norton, 2003.

Thomas, Evan. *The Very Best Men: Four Who Dared, the Early Years of the CIA.* New York: Touchstone Books/ Simon & Schuster, 1996.

Thomas, Hugh. *Cuba or the Pursuit of Freedom.* New York: Da Capo Press, 1998.

Thomas, Hugh. *Rivers of Gold: The Rise of the Spanish Empire, from Columbus to Magellan.* New York: Random House, 2003.

Valenti, Peter. *Errol Flynn: A Bio-Bibliography.* Westport, CT.: Greenwood Press, 1984.

Wills, Garry. *Nixon Agonistes: The Crisis of the Self-Made Man.* Boston: Mariner Books/Houghton Mifflin, 2002.

Wyden, Peter. *Bay of Pigs: The Untold Story.* New York: Simon & Schuster, 1979.

Yablonsky, Lewis. *George Raft.* San Francisco: Mercury House, 1974.

INDEX